Grade 5

PRACTICE READERS
VOLUME 2: UNITS 3 & 4

PEARSON

Glenview, Illinois • Boston, Massachusetts • Chandler, Arizona • Upper Saddle River, New Jersey

ISBN-13: 978-0-328-79575-8
ISBN-10:   0-328-79575-5
2 3 4 5 6 7 8 9 10 V0B4 17 16 15 14 13

Table of Contents

America

by Vera Cimarusti

Endings -ed, -ing, -s

allowed	Indians	sailed
Americas	invented	sailing
arrived	Islands	sailors
being	lived	seafarers
blowing	looked	shipping
called	looking	ships
continents	mapmakers	shores
countries	maps	spices
days	meats	spotted
determined	medicines	supplies
developed	named	technologies
Europeans	nations	thousands
expanded	needed	times
explorations	opened	traveling
explorers	perfumes	triangle-shaped
forced	places	uncharted
goods	producing	used
granted	returned	ways
helped	riches	years
hoped	routes	

In 1492, Christopher Columbus and his crew, looking for a sea route to Asia, sailed west in three ships across the Atlantic.

For thousands of years the major countries of the world had very little contact with each other. This all began to change as Western Europe and China began to send out explorers to learn about the world around them. As a result of their explorations, trade between Europe and Asia developed and expanded. Trade routes opened up. Nations began shipping their goods to faraway places.

In the 1300s, spices from Asia were in high demand in Europe. Europeans used them to flavor food and preserve meats. Europeans also used the spices in medicines and perfumes. Overland routes to Asia were long and dangerous. It was expensive to transport the goods to market too. European seafarers were looking for more efficient ways to trade with Asia. They hoped to find a sea route that would enable them to avoid overland routes.

New technologies were being developed that helped make sailing safer. The Chinese invented the compass, which allowed sailors to track the direction they were traveling in. Mapmakers were producing more accurate maps. Another invention that allowed sailors to travel farther out to sea was the triangle-shaped sail. This new sail allowed ships to travel in any direction, not just in the direction the wind was blowing.

Ships could travel east to Asia by sailing around the southern tip of Africa. This route was very dangerous, however. Italian Christopher Columbus was determined to find a new and safer route to Asia by sailing west. Columbus thought that if he sailed west he could circle the globe and arrive in Asia.

For seven years, Columbus looked for someone to finance his journey. Finally, in August of 1492, King Ferdinand and Queen Isabella of Spain granted Columbus the supplies, sailors, and ships he needed to carry out his expedition. He was given three sailing ships: the Niña, the Pinta, and the Santa Maria.

Even with the new technologies, the journey was still dangerous and uncharted. The sailors on Columbus's ships were afraid that they would be lost at sea. As the days aboard ship wore on, the sailors began to turn against Columbus. They forced him to agree to turn back if they did not find land within three days.

On the night of the second day, a lookout spotted land. Soon the explorers arrived on the shores of an island in the Caribbean. They named the island Hispañolia. Columbus thought he was in India, so he called the people who lived on the islands Indians. He did not realize he had arrived in part of the world previously unknown to the Europeans.

Although Columbus sailed to the Americas four times, the American continents were not named in his honor. Instead, in 1507, a German mapmaker named the continents in honor of another Italian explorer, Amerigo Vespucci.

Columbus returned to the Americas three more times. Each time he was in search of the mainland of India. Columbus never fully understood that he had opened a new land with great riches to European exploration.

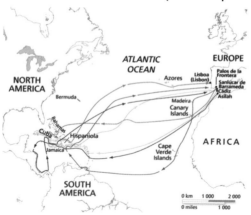

The map shows the routes for Columbus's four round-trip voyages west—1492–1493 (red), 1493–1496 (yellow), 1498–1500 (green), and 1502–1504 (blue).

Coral Reefs

by Felicia Jones

Endings -ed, -ing, -s

animals	growing	scientists
areas	grows	sea anemones
called	hundreds	seeking
colonies	joined	skeletons
composed	layers	soft-bodied
concerned	living	structures
constructed	located	supporting
creatures	nutrients	thousands
disappearing	organisms	waters
ecosystems	polyps	ways
endangered	reefs	years
environments	related	
forming	running	

Coral reefs are huge under-the-sea limestone structures. Tiny animals called coral polyps have constructed the reefs over many hundreds or even thousands of years. The hard coral forming a reef is composed of many layers of skeletons.

Coral polyps are soft-bodied organisms related to sea anemones. Living in colonies, the coral polyps create the skeletons to protect themselves. Without the skeletons, they would be prey for other sea creatures.

Over time colonies have joined with other colonies to form the reefs. Some coral reefs may have begun growing over 50 million years ago.

Most coral reefs are located in tropical waters. Coral grows best in warm, shallow waters where sunlight can reach the algae that the coral polyps depend on for nutrients. Coral polyps thrive in salt water. They are not found in coastal areas where fresh river water is running into the ocean.

Coral reefs teem with life, supporting about 25 percent of all marine creatures. Today, however, coral reefs are among the world's most endangered ecosystems. Scientists are concerned about these fragile environments. They are seeking ways to keep the reefs from disappearing.

Superheroes

by Jared Rosin

Endings -ed, -ing, -s

adopted	helped	rescued
called	imaginations	robbed
comic books	informed	screens
created	injustices	stopped
creators	Kents	superpowers
crimes	landing	theaters
developed	lived	using
discovered	learned	walls
enduring	naming	wearing
envisioned	needed	willing
fans	pages	worked
fearing	parents	
going	powers	

From the pages of comic books to the big screens at movie theaters, superheroes are part of our popular culture. Superman has been one of the most enduring superheroes. He was created by Jerry Siegel and Joe Schuster in 1933. They gave their superhero extraordinary powers to defend peace and justice. Fearing little other than kryptonite that robbed him of his powers, Superman stopped crimes and rescued those in danger. Using his X-ray vision, he could see through walls to detect trouble. Wearing his red cape, he could fly wherever he was needed. Always willing to fight against injustices, he helped the police solve and prevent crimes.

Superman lived among the people of Metropolis as Clark Kent. No one knew Clark Kent was Superman. Clark worked as a newspaper reporter. He was well informed about police activity.

Clark was not originally from Earth. He came from the planet Krypton. His parents learned that their planet was going to explode. They sent their infant son to Earth in a spaceship. After crash landing on Earth, the spaceship was discovered by the Kents. They adopted the child, naming him Clark. Over time, Clark's superpowers developed, and the Kents called him Superman.

Superman has become a most popular character since the 1930s. Surely his creators could not have envisioned how their superhero would capture the imaginations of fans around the world.

Horse Sense

by Jake Seldin

This sculpture shows Zeus, the king of the gods in Greek myth.

Suffixes -ly, -ian

absolutely	Grecian	Olympian
academician	immediately	really
actually	lazily	relentlessly
authoritarian	librarian	thoughtfully
equestrians		

Diego looked up thoughtfully from his textbook, where he was reading about a Grecian myth. It was warm at the seashore, and the waves were rolling in relentlessly until they ended up in a frothy crest. Once the crest crashed down, what was left of the wave would lap lazily to the shore. The sequence never stopped.

"No wonder the Greeks thought the sea-god Poseidon created the horse," Diego said, using his imagination. "The crests of those waves really look like white horse's manes!"

Seated across from Diego under the beach umbrella, Rajan immediately looked up the Greek Olympian gods online. "This Web site says that the Greeks believed there were lots of immortal horses. What do you think about doing our report about Olympian horses?"

"That's a great idea," Peter agreed, "and we can look up lots of information online. Diego, what Greek gods are mentioned in the stories in our textbook?"

"Let's start with Zeus, who is the king of the gods. Do you want to take that one, Rajan? And Peter, if you would you take Poseidon, I'll make a list of other mythological gods mentioned in the textbook."

It didn't take long for Rajan and Peter to find answers. "Wow," said Rajan, "the ancient storytellers were very creative. This Web page says the four Wind Gods drew Zeus's chariot in the shape of horses: Boreas was the North Wind, Notos was the South Wind, Zephyros was the West Wind, and Euros was the East Wind.

"Do you suppose Europe got its name because the East Wind blows in its direction?"

"I'm no academician," said Diego, "but we can ask the librarian how to find the answer. If it's true, it would be an interesting point to make in class, so please print out a map showing Europe's location."

Peter raised his eyebrows. "Zeus may be the king of the gods, but he wasn't much of an authoritarian. He allowed others to have power and respect. For example, Poseidon's eight horses absolutely outclassed Zeus's horses."

"What do you mean?" Diego asked.

This sculpture shows Poseidon, brother of Zeus and Greek god of the sea.

""He let Poseidon have eight horses, kept in a stable under the sea. Four had fish tails to get around in the ocean, and dolphins swarmed on either side of Poseidon's chariot, bowing to him in respect. They looked alive, they but were actually solid silver."

"Diego, who else should we look up?" Rajan asked.

Diego handed over his list, and Rajan and Peter split the names to research further. Peter went first: "The war god Ares had fire-breathing horses, but not all gods had horses. Aphrodite's chariot was drawn by doves, Artemis had four deer with gold horns, and Apollo sometimes used swans."

"It doesn't sound as though the Greek gods were avid equestrians," said Rajan. "None of them rode the horses, they just drove them." He turned around his computer so that they could see a picture on the monitor. "I wouldn't want to ride this one. It's a rooster in front and a horse in back."

Now Peter was laughing. "What is so funny?" Diego asked.

"Well, I was looking up the root word for *horse* and saw *horseradish*. Wouldn't you know that horseradish was often found growing near the sea!"

Kelvin, Boy Engineer

by Mike Temple

Suffixes *-ly, -ian*

Bostonian	fully	mathematician
certainly	guardians	scholarly
completely	intellectually	snugly

In 2010, when Kelvin Doe was just thirteen, he was already inventing things he needed. He had to. Money was short, and items such as off-the-shelf batteries were far too expensive to buy in his northwestern African home of Sierra Leone. So Kelvin figured out how to make his own batteries with what he could find at home: acid, soda, and metal. He put these into a tin cup and wrapped tape snugly around it. After a few misses, his battery worked!

Next he built a generator, which he made out of a voltage stabilizer he fished out of a dustbin, a motor, plug, and other components he found at home or in the garbage. In other words, he used what people often call junk. This junk, however, went into a generator that powered not just his home but also the mobile phone batteries of his neighbors. Kelvin even added his own FM radio station, which was fully equipped with a recycled CD player and a music mixer. The antenna he devised allowed the whole neighborhood to tune in to hear his broadcasts.

While these inventions are impressive, what's most amazing is that Kelvin didn't have any instruction to produce them. He was completely self-taught: no physicist, mathematician, or coach of any sort helped him. He is a genius.

Sierra Leoneans like Kelvin are the guardians of his country's future. At age sixteen, he was invited to the "Visiting Practitioner's Program" at the prestigious Massachusetts Institute of Technology (MIT) in Boston. Up until then he had never been more than ten miles away from his village. His Bostonian audience was riveted.

Scholarly opportunities like this will help ensure that Kelvin and other intellectually exceptional youth from his nation can contribute to its development and prosperity. Certainly in his small community, Kelvin was able to keep the lights on, all by himself.

Go to Your Own Room

by Ana Romano

Suffixes -ly, -ian

constantly	historians	newly
daily	immensely	strangely
electricians	musicians	

Long ago most homes didn't have anything like our plumbing, so there were no plumbers. There was no electricity, and no electricians. But historians tell us live musicians were enjoyed in the homes of the past.

Musicians would perform in the house's single major room: the great hall. The only other rooms were a kitchen and some little rooms off to the side. The great hall was kept warm by a fire in an open hearth. Smoke was supposed to go up a hole in the roof above the hearth. However, the room was often smoky, and the ceiling was blackened with soot. The family watched the hearth constantly. If fire broke out, there were no firefighters to help.

The average home did not have beds or bedrooms. Before sleeping, a family would "make a bed," a new one daily. There were no other beds and no bedrooms. Some families rolled out cloth pallets around the open hearth to sleep on. Others just heaped some newly gathered, fresh straw where they wanted to sleep and put a blanket on top.

When chimneys appeared, the air above the great hall improved immensely, and people developed a new idea: the upstairs. Bedrooms and studies were added. No smoke or sparks would rise into them, and people now had a place to sleep, read, visit, or just be alone.

Perhaps the most unusual reason for adding a room to the home involved the dining room. Strangely the dining room was not added to give the family a place to eat. It was created after upholstered furniture became popular in homes a little over 200 years ago. Till then everybody ate in the living room, on the "good furniture." Diners were wiping their fingers on the upholstery. No wonder they were sent to their own room!

Puerto Rico's El Yunque

by Elsa Sepulveda

El Yunque National Forest in Puerto Rico is part of the United States National Forest System.

Suffix -ize

minimized	popularized	theorized
mobilized	specialize	

17

El Yunque National Forest in Puerto Rico is located in the rugged range of the Sierra de Luquillo. It is the only tropical forest in the U.S. National Forest System. This treasure is one of the oldest reserves in the Western Hemisphere.

Today El Yungue National Forest is a wildlife refuge with hundreds of species of trees and plants. Twenty-six of the plant species are found nowhere else. Animals in the forest include turtles, frogs, birds, and more. The beautiful Puerto Rican parrot is one of them. This bright-green bird, with its red forehead and blue primary wing feathers, was once a common sight on the island. Today It is on the endangered species list.

Scientists who specialize in the study of rain forests have mobilized to save El Yungue National Forest. El Yunque mountain is part of this study. Usually covered in clouds and mist, El Yonque mountain lies entirely inside El Yunque National Forest. It rises high above the rivers, streams, crags, waterfalls, trees, ferns, and wildflowers of the forest. It is a stark, flat mountain.

No one knows for sure how El Yunque got its name. Some say it came from the name of an ancient Native American leader. Others say it is from the Native American spirit Yuquiye, meaning "Forest of Clouds."

In Spanish *el yunque* means "the anvil." This popularized translation is appropriate. Instead of being covered with plant life, like most rain forest landforms, El Yonque is practically barren. Few plants grow there.

Not only is the source of El Yunque's name a mystery. The mountain is also a mystery because of its slow erosion. Scientists say erosion is usually much faster on tropical mountaintops. El Yunque mountain doesn't follow the rule. It has a very slow erosion rate.

Because of the climate of the region, one would expect El Yunque to erode quickly. Trade winds sweep across El Yunque mountain constantly. It is often slammed by hurricanes. It stands in what is said to be the rainiest of all U.S. national forests. Rain pours down on the mountain an average of three times each day. Every year El Yunque National Forest's highest elevations receive more than 250 inches of rain. It is estimated that the entire forest receives 160 billion gallons of rain each year. Precipitation and wind are two factors that cause erosion.

The now endangered Puerto Rican parrot lives in El Yunque National Forest.

Some Puerto Rican areas have eroded about 1.6 to 3.2 inches since the late 1400s, but El Yunque Mountain has eroded only 0.08 inches in the same time. This would equal only about 13 feet every million years.

As the forest changes, scientists have questioned why the mountain has endured practically unchanged. They have theorized about why erosion to its rocks has been minimized on the mountain.

El Yunque mountain is what remains of Hato Puerco, an ancient supervolcano that existed over 145 million years ago. The volcano was one of the biggest and most active volcanos in this area. The part that is today called El Yunque mountain cooked within the volcano's chamber, becoming superhard.

Other rocks in the area didn't have the same superheating. They are softer and are more apt to break down from erosion and chemicals. So even if the rain forest disappears, El Yunque mountain will probably survive nearly unchanged for millions of years to come.

The Englishman's Fly

by Greg Salvo

Suffix -ize

capitalize	optimized	utilized
materialized	realized	

In 1983 the honeybee became Utah's official state insect because a fifth-grade class lobbied for its adoption. The insect is especially important to Utah because it is part of Utah's original name: The Provisional State of Deseret. *Deseret* means "honeybee."

Honey and honeycombs have been utilized for thousands of years. The ancient Egyptians used honey as perfume and the wax from the honeycomb in their burials. But when Christopher Columbus landed in the Americas, there were no honeybees. How they materialized in the Americas is an unsolved mystery. Did the explorers or colonists purposely bring bees to the Americas? If so, how did they keep the bees alive for the many weeks it took to sail to the Americas. Perhaps the honeybee was a stowaway that unintentionally arrived in the Americas.

Native Americans did not welcome the honeybee because they soon realized that wherever honeybees showed up, colonists were close behind. They called it "The Englishman's Fly." One account from Missouri says an Osage village held a day of mourning after finding a swarm of honeybees.

American lands, however, welcomed the bees. Forests had countless hollow tree trunks for the bees' nests, and lush prairie flowers offered an endless supply of nectar. Colonists soon learned to capitalize on their honey-producing insects, and new terms entered the English language.

Bee hunters set out sweet treats to attract the bees and followed their *beelines* to the nests. They gathered the sweet honey and sold it. *Yellow boy* molded wax cakes were used along with deer hides instead of money.

In this way the honeybee optimized the economy of more than one colonial settlement. Perhaps the only creatures that benefited more from the arrival of honeybees were the brown and black bears that became honey lovers.

Friends Forever

by Alana Mosher

Suffix -ize

fertilize   realize   scrutinized

organize   recognized

Latisha and Barbara sat on the warm grass, looking at the new seed packets. It was spring—time to plant vegetables as they did each year. Latisha scrutinized the gleaming new gardening tools: a spade, a hoe, and a hand rake. They made her realize change was good and bad.

This was the last year the girls would garden together because Latisha's family was moving away. She would love their new house, but she would miss the old neighborhood and Barbara especially. The family's apartment was near school, and Latisha had many friends, including Barbra, living right in the building.

Working in this garden was making Latisha sad. She liked spending her time in the garden with Barbara, but she would be far away in another city when the best part happened, harvesting the crop.

Barbara's older brother Stuart had always helped them organize, and he had already turned over the soil. "Did you fertilize?" Barbara asked. He had, so the girls started making furrows in the dirt to plant their pepper, cucumber, squash, and bean seeds row by row. Barbara noticed her friend's sad mood.

"What's wrong, Latisha?" she asked.

"Oh, nothing," Latisha said, but something was wrong! Latisha recognized that just as they had replaced the old tools with new ones, Barbara would replace her with a new gardening friend.

Stuart took a photo of the girls with his smart phone. "I'll e-mail it to you, Latisha." A week later Latisha's family arrived at their new home. Shortly after arriving in the new home, Latisha checked her e-mail, and there was the photo from Stuart with the message, "See your snail mail."

On the porch of the new home was a package for her. She opened it and out fell the old garden tools, four seed packets, and a note from Barbara: "Think of me when you plant and harvest these. You will always be my best friend."

The Art of Laughter

by James Toczlowski

Prefixes *com-, epi-, pro-*

committed	epicenter	products
complained	episode	proficient
complete	proclaimed	promise
composed	productions	pronounced

In our family, you have to be proficient in some art—that is, you have to be an artist. You might say my older brothers and sister are a hard act to follow. David, the oldest, has studied piano for eight years and is committed to being a concert pianist. He has even composed music to play at recitals. Gary, my other brother, is a masterful gymnast, and he has the medals to prove it. Those intricate moves on the parallel bars seem to come naturally to him. And then there is Elise, who is just a year older than me. She chose ballet and has danced gracefully off into *The Nutcracker* and other local productions to solid applause. Her teachers say she shows great promise. You can see how much pressure I am under.

Don't think I haven't tried to find my genius—but my adventures with the accordion, magic, tap dancing, and drums were complete disasters.

"The talent genes ran out before you got to me," I complained to my parents after my singing career proved a pronounced failure. "Not only am I tone deaf, but apparently I can't carry a tune in a bucket."

"Oh, James," Mom smiled at me, "you have worlds of talent. You just need time to discover it. Think about what you love doing."

I was plunked down at the kitchen table, the epicenter of family activity, noodling with a book report assignment. That got me thinking. I am a standout when it comes to humor. I am, as Dad is fond of saying, "the hammiest of hams." It's a cold day in July when I can't get everybody at the dinner table laughing over some silliness. And I apparently have a very good memory, since I have memorized every episode of my favorite cartoon show.

Comedy isn't art, I thought, but I definitely can give it my all. Then, in a flash, I had an inspiration for my book report on *A Wrinkle in Time*. I would make it a script for a talk show, and the host (yours truly) would interview Meg and her brother. For example, I could ask them about which laundry products helped them smooth out those wrinkles. I was off to the races!

That script had them rolling in the aisles of Ms. Duncan's reading class. Encouraged, I decided to enter the play-writing contest I saw advertised in *Comic Monthly*. "Submit your e-file manuscript of a one-act comedy by August 15. Winner and runner up will be published in next summer's edition," it proclaimed. A national publication would be awesome. I let myself daydream about the Sir James fan club that would no doubt result from my fame. Since the deadline was April 15, just a month and a half away, it was time to get writing!

When I finished on April 14, I was certain "As the Hound Howls" was a masterpiece. My takeoff on a soap opera for the doggy set had made my family laugh until tears ran down their cheeks. With fingers crossed, I attached the file to my submission e-mail and pressed "Send." Now there was nothing to do but wait.

Or so I thought. It seems word of my comedy writing has traveled. The drama club at Harrison Middle School has asked me to write a script for their spring play. I have some ideas to talk over with them.

As my mind circled puns, sight gags, and slapstick, I had this thought: Maybe comedy really IS an art. Maybe anything you do can be art if you take it to the highest level.

Ads Everywhere

by Abigail McNabb

Prefixes *com-, epi-, pro-*

commercials	epidemic	product(s)
companions	produces	profoundly
complexes		

Have you ever considered how profoundly you are affected by advertising? In every aspect of our lives and every part of our day, advertisements are our constant companions.

It's estimated that the average American watches about 100 television ads a day. A few TV channels even broadcast nothing but commercials.

In magazines and papers, on billboards, in buses, on clothing, on the fences and walls of sports complexes— advertisements bombard us with their clamor to "Buy! Buy now! Buy more!" Once found mostly in print, radio, and television, ads have now taken over every thinkable space around us. Even at the movies, products are placed strategically on the screen and advertised through the script.

The epidemic of advertisements has spread like wildfire on the Internet. It is practically impossible to visit a Web site that isn't jumbled with ads, many of them flashing or dancing to get our attention. Lack of regulation also has meant that Internet ads can lurk within supposedly factual stories. For example, a company that produces medicines may sponsor a medical site and include articles or studies favorable to its products. In addition, Internet ads are actually using up your computer's resources as they distract you.

This ad-mania, from logos to labels, means we are exposed to thousands of ads daily. They whisper, scream, sing, and cajole to persuade us that we can't live without the product of the moment. It's enough to make you want to get away from it all for a while. That's a good idea. But first a word from our sponsor. . . .

The Best Last Words

By Pat Avary

Prefixes com-, epi-, pro-

commemorates	composition	epitaph(s)
communicated	compresses	profile
compact	epilogue	

For a writer, it can be the most important composition of a lifetime. For anyone, it is the "last word" communicated to others. An epitaph is a statement that commemorates the life of a person. Often epitaphs appear on tombstones.

An epitaph deserves to be carefully considered, for it creates a profile. It gives the final impression of who this person was. It compresses much meaning into a small space. If you think of a life as a play, the epitaph is the epilogue. It returns to the "stage" to sum up what the play was about. So, the epitaph is compact—short and sweet enough to fit on a granite block.

A comedian may choose to leave us laughing. Consider the comic Spike Milligan. He was famous for his bold humor. His epitaph says, "I told you I was sick."

Some people express their pride in what they accomplished. Pi is a number showing the ratio of a circle's circumference to its diameter. It is the same for any circle. The mathematician who first calculated the value of pi, Ludolph von Ceulen, put this on his epitaph: "3.14159265358973238462643383279 50."

Studs Terkel was an energetic author and radio personality who lived ninety-six years. He remained curious and active far longer than most. His epitaph reads, "Curiosity did not kill this cat."

Then there is Mel Blanc, the "Man of a Thousand Voices." Blanc created the voices for cartoon characters such as Bugs Bunny, Porky Pig, Yosemite Sam, Woody Woodpecker, and Sylvester the Cat. His epitaph may be the cleverest of all. It says simply, "That's all folks!"

The Greatest Athlete

by Wallis Lindell

Babe Didrickson won the hurdle event at the 1932 Olympics in Los Angeles.

Idioms

as a duck takes to water	in a heartbeat	slammers
as a rule of thumb	in the limelight	standout
fell in love	put stock in	to boot
	reach for the stars	

Many people reach for the stars, but very few actually make it. One dreamer who achieved every goal she set for herself was Babe Didrickson Zaharias. She mastered more than a dozen sports and won Olympic medals as well as many championships, tournaments, and awards. As an amateur and as a professional athlete, Babe was nothing less than a story-book champion.

Mildred Didrickson was born in 1914 in Texas. She earned the nickname "Babe" (after Babe Ruth) when she hit five slammers over the fence in a childhood baseball game. Babe was the only girl playing in that game.

Her early years were hard times for the family, so Babe contributed to the family by working various part-time jobs. Her father put so much stock in physical conditioning that he built weight-lifting equipment. This helped Babe grow strong.

Babe loved competition and joined often in the games her brothers played. She took to whatever sport she tried as a duck takes to water. She was such a standout in high school basketball that at fifteen, she was asked to join the Golden Cyclones, one of the best women's basketball teams in the country. For the next three years, the team won the national championship each year.

Next, Babe turned her attention to track and field. In a heartbeat, she was winning the events she entered. In less than two years, she qualified for the Olympic Games. As a rule of thumb, it's a team that wins.

But Babe earned 30 points all by herself, while the runner-up *team* scored just 22. Babe competed in eight of the ten scheduled events. She won five events, setting world records in the javelin, 80-meter hurdles, high jump, and baseball throw.

The Los Angeles Olympics that year would place Babe in the limelight of world-class athletics. Limited to three events, she prevailed in all of them. She won the javelin throw and set a world record in the 80-meter hurdles. She tied for gold in the high jump.

Looking for a new challenge, she turned to golf in 1933. Soon, as you might expect, she was winning championships and dominating the game.

In 1938, Babe met George Zaharias, a wrestler with whom she fell in love. They married eleven months later, but marriage did not slow Babe Didrickson Zaharias's march to golfing history.

At 145 pounds, Babe was no heavyweight, but she routinely drove the ball 250 yards. When asked how she could do this, she said, "You've got to . . . let it rip." She was named the American Press Female Athlete of the Year in 1945, 1946, and 1947. She turned pro in 1947, after winning seventeen of eighteen tournaments. In 1948, Babe won golf's U.S. Women's Open, the World Championship, and the All-American Open. In 1950, she was named Woman Athlete of the Half Century.

Babe continued to dominate the women's professional golf tour for several more years. In 1953, Babe learned she had cancer. Despite her illness, the next year she won the U.S. Women's Open and five more titles to boot, in addition to her sixth American Press Female of the Athlete of the Year award.

In 1955, pain prevented Babe from competing any longer and in September 1956, she died. However, the legend of Babe Didrickson Zaharias lives on. As a teenager she had said her goal was "to be the greatest athlete who ever lived." There are many who would say that she succeeded.

Eat Well to Live Well

by Shelley Wallis

Idioms

all the fuss about	holy grail	peaks and valleys
bottom line	lucky for us	star power
by the way	nothing could be further from the truth	

Why do adults always talk about the idea of "eating right"? The body you are building can only be as good as what you put into it. Growing bodies require good nutrition. This means eating enough foods with the right nutrients.

Lucky for us, today we know what nutrients we need for energy, health, and growth, and we also know which foods have the most star power to meet these goals. To thrive, the human body needs carbohydrates, fats, proteins, water, fiber, vitamins, and minerals. The holy grail of nutrition consists of getting the right combination of these nutrients.

Drinking enough water is the bottom line; water is essential to every function and every cell in the body. By the way, few Americans drink enough water.

What is all the fuss about good carbs versus bad carbs? Carbohydrates provide the fuel to keep our bodies running. Whole fruits and vegetables and whole grains provide the best source of "good carbs," fiber, vitamins, and minerals. Too often, however, we get most of our carbs from foods filled with refined white flour and sugar. This provides lots of calories but not many nutrients. The result can be peaks and valleys of energy and obesity.

For good protein, which helps your body build muscle, think lean meats, fish, eggs, nuts, and dairy. It's smart to limit fatty meats. Some people think that they should avoid all fat, but nothing could be further from the truth. A balanced diet gets 10 to 20 percent of its calories from healthy fats. Good fats are found in foods such as olive oil, avocados, and nuts.

Remember, eating right means eating a balanced diet. Choose a healthful diet with delicious, nutritious foods.

Towers in the Sky

By Winnie Bemis

Idioms

came up with	ruled out	took advantage of
for good	taken over	wound up
made a difference	tall order	

Today, we are used to dramatic city skylines with skyscrapers rising to the clouds. But skyscrapers have only existed since the 1880s. Before that, tall buildings—always made of stone—were a tall order. This building material was strong but ruled out thin walls and large openings. The towers and cathedrals built centuries ago wound up with few windows and dark interiors.

In time, steel made from iron became widely available. Builders took advantage of the metal's strength. They came up with a strong skeleton of steel columns and beams. This steel "backbone" helped the building resist the wind. That strength also made a difference in the light a building could admit. Many windows could be installed on each floor. The invention of the elevator also helped make skyscrapers possible. (After all, few people want to climb thousands of stairs!)

In the 1880s, these elements came together in the first skyscraper. The Home Insurance Building in Chicago rose a whopping ten stories. By the 1940s, skyscrapers had taken over the urban skyline for good. However, the average skyscraper was just 200 feet tall.

Today, new structural designs permit construction of skyscrapers fifty times stronger and much taller. The world's tallest buildings soar 1,500 feet or more into the air. Builders experiment with new styles and methods. The skylines of many cities boast a fantastic variety of shapes and gleaming surfaces. Wouldn't ancient builders be amazed at the sight!

Amazing Spiders

by Juanita Hernandez

Synonyms

abilities, skills

amazing, remarkable

arachnid(s), spider(s)

copy, decoy, fake

creatures, organisms

dislike, phobia

generates, produce

hunt, prey on

prey, victim

poisoning, venomous

41

Many people have a phobia about spiders. The sight of an arachnid is enough to make them shudder and scramble away. Human dislike of these eight-legged creatures may have grown out of our ancient survival instincts. Almost all spiders are venomous, to some degree. Avoiding them may have saved our ancestors from poisoning that causes injury or even death. However, we also have a fascination with arachnids, for these organisms, which are so unlike us, have remarkable skills.

Some of those abilities exist to help spiders hunt. All spiders prey on other small creatures, such as insects and worms. A few large spiders such as tarantulas can even take down larger organisms such as birds and lizards. Two abilities make spiders successful hunters. They can spin silk and turn a victim into liquid.

From birth to death, all spiders can produce silk. A spider's body generates the silk, and the spider pulls it out of spinnerets, or openings, with its hind legs. It uses the superstrong fibers to capture lunch, provide shelter, move from place to place, and protect eggs.

A spider web is a masterful bug trap. To be sure, not all spiders spin webs. For example, wolf spiders stalk their prey, and jumping spiders pounce on theirs. However, most spiders construct webs, carrying their own construction materials inside them. They also create the intricate shape again and again. Spider webs are strong, but they still need to be constantly replaced.

So the spider eats its web, recycles the silk, and creates a brand new web.

The spider not only engineers the complex design for its web, it also makes some parts sticky and some nonsticky. The frame is constructed of nonstick silk to allow pathways for building and moving around the web. The radius threads are coated with a sticky material for catching bugs.

Although the spider is a predator, it cannot chew and swallow its prey. Arachnids are unable to digest solid foods. Instead, spiders liquefy their dinner. Some push digestive enzymes onto the victim's body. These chemicals break the prey's internal organs down into juice which the spider can suck up. Other spiders inject venom that turns the insides of a captured insect into a watery soup.

Many people find the spider's eight eyes creepy. Nevertheless, all four pair of peepers help the arachnid. One central pair of eyes provides sharp color vision for seeing details. Secondary pairs detect motion, alerting the spider when something dangerous is coming.

New discoveries are being made all the time, and they reveal even more amazing spider abilities. For example, in 2012, scientists discovered a tiny spider in the rainforest of Peru. First, they saw a web with what looked like a large spider in the center. Close inspection showed that this shape was actually a decoy. The real spider had built a copy of a spider from debris encased in silk. The fake had eight legs and two body parts, like any spider. The tiny spider at the top vibrated the web to make the decoy look threatening. It makes one wonder: Can spiders count? Can they think?

Spiders may draw you in with their fascinating skills or send you running in terror. Either way, you must admit that there is much to admire in the arachnid world.

Ridding the Ocean of Garbage

By Paul Weston

Synonyms

answer, solution

clean up, get rid of, remove

concept, idea

enormous, huge, vast

gadget, invention

garbage, trash, waste

Plastic trash is becoming the horror story of our oceans. Enormous quantities of our castoff plastic bottles, wraps, and containers wind up in the ocean. Since plastic does not break down, it winds up killing millions of aquatic animals. It also pollutes the water and animals that eat it with harmful chemicals.

Our vast oceans now contain so much garbage that huge floating trash heaps, called gyres, have appeared. Clearly, we need to find ways to reduce our plastic waste. However, we also must find a way to get rid of these floating garbage patches.

One teenager thinks he has found a solution. Many scientists believe he has the answer, too. At 19, Boyan Slat invented an Ocean Cleanup Array. (An array is an arrangement of parts that work as a unit.) Slat's invention combines floating booms, or connected pieces to catch floating objects, with anchored platforms. The network of booms would be placed around garbage patches. They would work with ocean currents to funnel the trash into platforms. The platforms would serve as processers, collecting and separating the plastic trash. Then the garbage would be removed and recycled.

Slat's idea began with a paper he wrote for school in 2012. It was widely praised and given awards. After the young man further developed his concept, the Ocean Cleanup Foundation signed on. They believe in the gadget enough that they are backing the research and seeking funding to make it a reality. Slat figures that in five years, the arrays could clean up a garbage gyre. It is believed they can remove 7,250,000 tons of plastic waste from the oceans.

Double Your Fun

By Jasper Jackson

Synonyms

amazing, awesome

authority, dominance

beat, bested

completed, finished

different, unlike

familiar, usual

habitually, usually

identical, same

Frances is thirty-five minutes older than Stanley. She uses this fact to assert her greater authority. But at age twelve, Stanley is an inch taller than Frances. So let's call the battle for dominance a tie. These twins have the same dark curly hair and identical brown eyes, and they are both stubborn to a fault (or so their parents claim). Otherwise, they are as different as night and day.

It's Friday night, and they are busy showing how unlike they can be.

"Video games?" queried Stan. Stanley usually beat his sister when they played electronics.

Fran shook her head, countering, "Scrabble tournament." Frances habitually bested her brother in word games.

Dad intervened, telling the twins it was their turn to clean up the kitchen after supper. When they were finished, he added, they had a surprise coming.

This was a familiar Friday chore that they had learned to streamline by teamwork. Fran rinsed dishes, and Stan loaded the dishwasher, as usual. Then while Stan wiped up the table, stove, and counters, Fran washed and dried the pots and pans. While they completed their task, they guessed what the surprise might be. As they finished, Mom held out tickets to the new science fiction movie they had both been dying to see.

"Oh, wow! Amazing!" whooped Fran.

"Awesome!" yelled Stan.

They headed for the movie theater happily arguing about which row in the theater was the best "of all time" for movie watching.

How to Be a Citizen of Change

by Pat Murphy

Volunteers paint a mural in a school.

Prefix _im-_

immature	imperfect	impossible
immeasurable	impersonal	impractical
impatient	impolite	

Young people might think they are too young to make a difference or contribute to society. They may think they are too young or immature to help bring about positive changes in their communities. However, that's simply not the case. In an imperfect world, even simple actions can help make a community a better place to live. Young people can find many opportunities to demonstrate good citizenship in their community, their country, and the world.

Start by learning about your community and thinking of ways you can be of service. Learn about your local government and the issues facing the community. If possible, attend or view meetings of your city council or school board. The information you learn from these meetings might help you identify an issue or a service that means a lot to you.

As you study issues and services, you may find that some are too large or impractical for you to tackle. Others, however, may be just perfect for you and your friends to take on. Perhaps you could help clean up a local park or paint a wall mural. Perhaps you can volunteer to visit hospital patients or do errands for senior citizens. The possibilities are endless.

Once you find an issue or a service that speaks to you, do research to find out more about it. Find out if your community has a group working on the issue or providing the service. If it doesn't, find out which government official, department, or organization you could contact about starting a project to help meet this need.

Once you have a contact, prepare a presentation to promote your project and your plan for achieving your goal. Creating a short presentation will help show you are serious and also help you organize your thoughts. Your plan should show your willingness to work with others and include ideas for interesting others in the project.

Once your plan is accepted of revised, it is time to begin working. Participate fully in the project and dedicate yourself to accomplishing your goal. At times throughout the project, you may have to work directly with the public. When dealing with the public, do not be impersonal or impolite, instead be friendly and courteous. This will demonstrate that you genuinely care about what you are doing to help your community. Remember that to earn respect, first you have to give it.

Volunteers clean up a community park.

While you work, keep your final goal in mind. Some goals may be long term, and to accomplish them, you may have to work for weeks, months, or even years. Don't get discouraged or be impatient. Consider breaking your big goal into smaller milestones that you can use to assess your progress.

If you suffer a setback, remind yourself that this is normal in everyday life. It is impractical to believe that you will accomplish everything easily. But if you keep your tasks reasonable and do not try to do the impossible, you should accomplish your goal. Just do your best and work hard. The rewards you will receive will be immeasurable.

Robots from Space

by Aaron Williams

Prefix im-

imbalance	immovable	impossible
immeasurable	impenetrable	improbable
immortal		

An incredible noise shattered the serenity of Tyler's afternoon, rocking the earth like a massive earthquake. The young boy looked up to see an improbable sight on the distant horizon—robots emerging from a spaceship! Towering above the treetops and dwarfing the nearby buildings, the robots were gigantic, colossal, and surely immeasurable. The robots looked like enormous humans, but the similarity ended there.

In the neighboring city, citizens piled into trucks and cars to face the threat the aliens posed. They planned to rid the city of the aliens, most likely an impossible task. When the trucks drew close to the aliens, the robots planted their feet firmly on the ground. As the mechanical beasts took a stance, they appeared to be substantial, intimidating, and immovable. The humans launched an assault, but the robots' impenetrable armor repelled all attacks.

Tyler realized the robots made masterful villains since they were mechanical and had computers for brains. They seemed almost immortal. Tyler recognized the imbalance in the powers of these automatons versus those of the humans. Suddenly, Tyler was startled in the middle of his musings when, a female robot's voice pierced the air, calling out his name.

"Tyler!" his mom called, "Have you finished your homework yet?" This broke Tyler's fantastic daydream. He loved creating stories, but Mom was correct; there was a time to daydream and a time to do homework. Tyler grinned and went back to writing his report, "My Ideal Career: Movie Director"!

When the Aliens Landed

by Mei Lin

Prefix *im-*

immaterial   impossible   improbable

immobile

Martians landed on Earth and began a war between the two worlds. Well, at least that's what many people thought. This "War of the World" was actually a radio show that was intended as a prank. The radio show *Mercury Theatre on the Air* broadcast the drama on October 30, 1938.

The play "War of the World" was based on a novel by H. G. Wells. To make it more believable, writers set the drama in New Jersey on the night of the broadcast. Also Orson Welles and the other actors performed the drama as a newscast. They did say at the beginning of the show that it was fiction. However, people who tuned in after the beginning didn't hear that warning.

The story starts out with the landing of a spacecraft from Mars. A crowd sees an immobile Martian inside. However, the Martian then fires a heat ray into the crowd, and the war begins. The story ends with "Isn't there anyone on the air? Isn't there . . . anyone?"

People should have realized it was a prank. After all, it was very improbable that there were aliens in the first place.

It should have seemed impossible to most people that there were aliens and that they came to Earth. Of course, many people easily believed that aliens would want to take over. It was immaterial that there were no other warnings of an invasion. It also didn't matter that there was no record of life on Mars. People still panicked when they heard the broadcast. Eventually, they found out it was just a joke. On that night, Orson Welles gained fame as a masterful storyteller and trickster.

Serving Your Country

by Natalie Roma

A Peace Corps worker in Africa talks with a family.

Acronyms

SEALs, Sea, Air, Land

UNICEF, United Nations International Children's Fund

VISTA, Volunteers in Service to America

WAC, Women's Army Corps (Army)

WAVES, Women Accepted for Volunteer Emergency Service (Navy)

Citizens of the United States enjoy many benefits that many other people do not have. In return, citizens are expected to be loyal to their country, to stay informed about important issues, and to vote in elections. But many U.S. citizens want to do more to serve their country. There are a number of ways they can choose to help.

One of the most obvious choices for service is the armed services. The U.S. military exists to protect the United States and its interests. Men and women who want to serve can choose among five branches: the Navy, Army, Air Force, Marines, and Coast Guard.

This was not always true for women, although a number of females served as nurses in military hospitals throughout our nation's history. Women could not enlist in any branch of the armed forces until World War II when the Army and Navy formed special corps for women. Women enlisted in the WACs (for the Army) and WAVES (for the Navy). They performed many noncombat tasks, from office work to machine mechanics. Today, women can enlist or train to be officers alongside men in the various branches of service.

Each branch of the military has divisions. For example, the Army, which is America's land-based military power, includes the Army and Army Reserve as well as the Army National Guard. Men and women in the National Guard give a portion of their time to service. They remain in their homes, but they train regularly and are called up to help in emergencies.

Sometimes, they are deployed overseas, just like regular military.

One special division of the Navy is the SEALs. They include hand selected, highly trained individuals who carry out special operations on sea, air, and land. These warriors generally work in small teams at night; they conduct some of our country's most important missions.

Besides the armed forces, Americans can serve in special organizations such as VISTA. This volunteer service organization was founded in 1965 to make a difference in the lives of poor Americans. VISTA members serve for one year. They may try to improve reading skills, health services, businesses, or many other conditions in poor communities.

A U.S. Navy Seal checks an instrument as he swims underwater.

The Peace Corps is a similar volunteer service organization at the international level. Its members serve for two years and may be posted anywhere in the world. In addition, the United Nations has a branch called UNICEF, which helps children around the world. These two organizations and others work to help children escape danger and violence, survive diseases, and gain an education.

All of the opportunities I have described are for adults. How can young people serve their country? They can volunteer in their own communities. For example, they can clean up litter, plant trees, and build community gardens. They can collect food for food banks or tutor younger students. Youths can and do visit nursing home patients and assist in public libraries. Many nonprofit organizations and charities rely on volunteers to do their good works.

There are many opportunities for service, at any age and in any part of the country. When you help your community, you help your country. Volunteering also has a selfish benefit: it makes you feel good! Serving others makes for a stronger, healthier community and at the same time makes you feel valuable and content.

Exploring Space

By Zach Quinn

Acronyms

NASA, National Aeronautics and Space Administration

POTUS, President of the United States

For centuries, human beings have pondered space. But even a hundred years ago, most people could not have imagined space travel. Today, NASA and other space agencies have engineered rockets, space shuttles, and a space station. They have sent up many satellites that enable instant world communication and monitor Earth's environments around the clock. Highly trained experts have blasted off into orbit and into deep space. They have walked on the moon and set up equipment to peer deep into the universe. NASA's robots now prowl the surface of Mars, probing its secrets and looking for signs of life.

With such exciting work, no wonder "How can I become an astronaut?" is among the agency's most frequently asked questions. Human beings are intrepid explorers. We are always pushing the boundaries of human knowledge and the known universe. Astronauts form perhaps the most elite group of adventurers the world has ever seen.

NASA's accomplishments were all achieved in fewer than sixty years. October 1, 1958, marks the official birth date of NASA. A few years later, then POTUS John F. Kennedy challenged NASA and inspired the nation to "commit itself to . . . [land] a man on the Moon and [return] him safely to Earth." This challenge was met by 1969.

As much as space exploration has advanced, it is still in its infancy. As people reach farther into space, they hope to learn if alien life forms actually do inhabit distant planets.

Having a Blast

By Jere Nois

Acronyms

ASAP, as soon as possible

NATO, North Atlantic Treaty Organization

radar, radio detecting and ranging

zip code, zone improvement plan code

To: Ozman
Subject: Your Visit and Our July 4 Party

Hi, Ozzie. How's my favorite cousin? It's hotter than a firecracker in Omaha, Nebraska. Speaking of fireworks, I can't wait for you to come to my family's Fourth of July party. I have my room all ready so you can share it with me that night.

I hope you and your folks can get here by noon. That's the kickoff for the Nois family water battle. Don't worry, we don't need to get NATO involved—this is a ruckus that everyone, adults and kids, enjoys because everyone gets splashed and cools off.

After that we have sack races, play baseball, and laze around in the shade until it is time for the cookout. By then, guests are starting to arrive with their yummy dishes to share. There will be so many cars parked in the driveway and on the street that you would think they stretch into the next zip code.

Mom and Dad have been getting ready all week. They will grill plenty of veggies and burgers and put out pitchers of cold lemonade and iced tea. The wonderful smells will draw everyone to the patio like radar. Mom makes this amazing flag cake covered with whipped cream, blueberries, and strawberries.

Then, after sunset, the fireworks begin in the park. We have a great view from our yard. The darkness fills up with explosions that look like a crazy bouquet of sizzling light-flowers. It's the most spectacular display you'll ever see, I promise.

Do you want to stay over an extra few days to go with us to the LogJam Water Park? My folks say it's fine, if your folks agree. Let me know ASAP if you can.

An Orderly Transition

by Meredith Sexton

At Rice University on September 12, 1962, President John F. Kennedy spoke about the challenges of peaceful space exploration.

Greek and Latin Roots

charisma	dynamic	negotiate
committee	encouraged	political
corps	government	prominent
country	inspired	registration(s)
crisis	investigate	segregation
democracy	legislation	Senate
discrimination		

When John F. Kennedy became the 35th President of the United States in 1961, Americans were inspired and hopeful. Kennedy came from a wealthy, prominent family in Massachusetts. He was youthful, only forty-three years old. He had ideas for doing amazing things, such as sending a man to the moon. He encouraged people to spread democracy throughout the world by starting the Peace Corps. (Peace Corps volunteers live in developing countries and help their citizens improve their way of life.) Kennedy motivated all Americans to take an active part in their government. He said, "Ask not what your country can do for you; ask what you can do for your country." Many Americans agreed that Kennedy had *charisma:* a dynamic personality that attracted their interest and loyalty.

President Kennedy's assassination on November 22, 1963, shocked and saddened Americans. Kennedy had barely had time to begin making the changes he had proposed. The new President was Lyndon B. Johnson, the Vice President. Lyndon Johnson was very different from John Kennedy. He had grown up in a very poor family in Texas. At fifty-four years old, he didn't project the youthful quality of Kennedy. Johnson had served in the House of Representatives for nearly twelve years and in the Senate for twelve years.

President Johnson's first job was to reassure Americans during and after the crisis of November 22. Johnson took the oath of office about two hours after

Kennedy was killed, and a photo of the event was widely published. Johnson announced that he would finish the projects that Kennedy had started. He quickly renamed NASA headquarters in Florida the John F. Kennedy Space Center. He also organized a committee to investigate Kennedy's assassination. Johnson's leadership helped Americans heal and feel that their country was returning to normal after Kennedy's murder.

Lyndon B. Johnson was the thirty-sixth President of the United States, serving from November 1963 through January 1969.

The most important goal of the new President was enacting the Civil Rights Bill into law. In June 1963, President Kennedy had proposed the Civil Rights Act of 1964. This legislation would outlaw racial discrimination such as segregation in schools and other public places. It would outlaw requiring different types of voter registrations for whites and for African Americans. Kennedy had worked on passing the bill before he died, but some Southern legislators were against it. President Johnson made the Civil Rights Bill a major priority. Johnson felt strongly that no American should be discriminated against. His many years of experience in Congress and his excellent political skills helped Johnson negotiate the bill's passage. He signed the bill into law on July 2, 1964. But Johnson wasn't done with improving Americans' civil rights. In 1965, he led the passage of the Voting Rights Act, which helped African Americans achieve equality in elections.

When President Kennedy was assassinated, the nation was fearful and heartbroken. His successor, President Johnson, helped America heal. He was a strong leader, and he completed some of the programs most dear to Kennedy's heart. The transition from the assassinated President to America's new leader was not only peaceful but positive in many ways.

A Budding Career

by Andrew Carlson

Greek and Latin Roots

administration	architect	equipment
agriculture	botany	noticed
annuals	ceremony	perennials
apologize	climate	vacant

Jared was leaving school one afternoon when he noticed his neighbor Mr. Wood working on a vacant patch on school property. "What are you working on?" he asked.

"Hello, Jared. The school administration asked me to make a garden out of this space so that students can relax and enjoy beautiful plants during lunch and recess."

Jared, who was fascinated by agriculture and botany, contemplated the work Mr. Wood had done so far. He said, "Did you consider using a sedge instead of grass to make upkeep easier? Also, maybe you could plant perennials in this corner instead of annuals that have to be replaced each year. Lavender would grow well in our climate, and it's very hardy. A Japanese cherry tree would be perfect in the center because we could enjoy the blossoms every spring. You might consider a wildflower garden in this area instead of these fussy zinnias and petunias, and if you laid some flagstones, kids could walk through the flowers and enjoy the scents." Jared realized that Mr. Wood was staring at him. "Sorry, Mr. Wood, but I love plants, and I have tons of gardening ideas."

"Don't apologize, Jared; I think you're just the partner I need." That night Mr. Wood and Jared consulted gardening software at Jared's house. They made a two-week schedule for buying plants and equipment, planting, and laying a path.

A month later Jared's school celebrated the fragrant, colorful new garden with a ceremony. The principal introduced Mr. Wood, who said, "Thanks for this delightful garden should go to Jared Brooks, our gifted landscape architect."

A Golden Symbol

by Mari Endo

Greek and Latin Roots

engineering	pedestrians	unpredictable
geometric	symbol	visible
ingenuity	transportation	

What landmark is practical, stylish, an engineering marvel, and a symbol of America? The Golden Gate Bridge in San Francisco fits this description.

The Golden Gate Bridge was begun in 1933 and completed in 1937. Area residents needed a route across the San Francisco Bay from San Francisco north to Marin County. Ferryboats had been the only way to cross for 100 years. The explorer John C. Frémont named this part of the bay the Golden Gate in 1846. Many thought a bridge could not be built here. The strait has very deep water, strong winds, and unpredictable fogs.

The bridge engineers chose a cable-suspension design. The roadway hangs from cables that go across towers. They are fastened at each end. This style is fitting for bridges that span a long distance, like the nearly 9,000 feet of the Golden Gate. The two towers are Art Deco, a popular 1930s style. It is marked by strong colors and geometric shapes. The towers are painted "International Orange," a color for which the bridge is known worldwide. Believe it or not, the bridge might have had black and yellow stripes. The Navy thought this pattern would make the bridge more visible to ships.

Today the Golden Gate Bridge is used by 110,000 cars per day. An unending parade of pedestrians also crosses the bridge daily. It is a symbol of American artistic style and ingenuity.

Ruthie the Riveter

by Judith Norton

During World War II, these women and others helped the war effort by building airplanes.

Complex Spelling Patterns

anxious	extraneous	perilous
cautious	glorious	righteous
	joyous	victorious

Ruth Ann had her life planned. After graduating from high school in June, she would attend the state college in town. Afterwards she would work as a secretary for a few years. Then, if she met the right person, she would get married, have children, and become a homemaker. But as a Scottish poet once said, "The best-laid plans of mice and men oft go astray." That's what happened to Ruth Ann's plans when the Japanese bombed Pearl Harbor in December 1941. It meant the United States was entering the World War that had been raging in Europe and Asia since 1939.

High school graduation was not as joyous as Ruth had foreseen. Unfortunately, most of the boys she graduated with temporarily gave up their plans for college or civilian jobs. They had to report for military service. They would train for a few weeks somewhere in the United States and then go to Europe or Asia. Ruth's older brother was already an Air Force pilot, stationed in England and making flights to Germany and France. Ruth hoped and prayed every day that he would come home from this perilous duty soon.

Just as she did before the war, Ruth spent her summer going to the town swimming pool and to the movies with friends. But even this was different, with all the young men missing. She tried to believe that life was normal, but the war had changed her community and her life.

One day Ruth was pulling weeds in her mom's vegetable garden when her friend Betty turned up. "Big news: you know the car factory in Springfield is making airplanes now, right? I just heard that they're advertising for girls to work in the factory! They need workers for the war effort, and they pay well—lots more than we could make in a store or an office."

Ruth had seen the signs in the news: illustrations of a young woman they called "Rosie the Riveter" doing factory work normally done by men. With many men at war and airplanes, tires, and other products needed for the war effort, the country was encouraging women to work in manufacturing plants.

Ruth's response was cautious. "We're going to college in September, Betty. My part-time job at the library is fine until then." Then Betty did what she always did, using her persuasive powers to convince Ruth that they should apply for jobs at the airplane factory.

During World War II, airplanes were used to fly bombing missions.

Before she knew it, Ruth was working on an assembly line. It was the hardest work she'd ever done, but it was also satisfying. Many girls she knew from school worked at the plant too, and they ate lunch together every day. She liked earning more money than she had ever earned before, and she put almost all of it into her savings account. New hats or dresses were extraneous in wartime. Last but not least, Ruth felt her actions were righteous. The airplanes she was helping to make might help the United States and the Allies be victorious.

When the summer ended, Ruth felt anxious about quitting her job and going to college. She had endless talks with her parents. Finally she made a decision: college could wait until the war ended or her work was not needed at the factory. If boys could postpone their plans because of the war, so could she.

After six months of work, Ruth had a job review by her supervisor. "You're an excellent worker, Ruth Ann, and I'm promoting you to supervisor. After you go to college, I hope you'll accept a permanent position." Ruth was secretly thrilled. It would be glorious for the war to end and the soldiers to come back safely. But for now, she would enjoy her career.

Marvelous High Line Park

by Len Onassi

Complex Spelling Patterns

ambitious	ingenious	precious
enormous	marvelous	various
harmonious	musicians	

America's cities have many splendid parks: Lincoln Park in Chicago, Mission Bay Park in San Diego, City Park in New Orleans. One of the country's newest city parks is also one of its most unusual.

The High Line in New York was an elevated freight railroad line built in the 1930s. Thirty feet off the ground, this railroad line ran from 34th Street to Spring Street. Manufactured products and foods were transported on the line, but by the 1950s, trucks more often delivered goods. Use of the High Line decreased, and in the 1980s, freight was transported on the High Line for the last time.

Area residents wondered what to do with an obsolete elevated railroad track that was nearly one and a half miles long. Some wanted to demolish it, but others started a group, Friends of the High Line. Their ingenious idea was to transform the precious city land into a public open space. They hired experts in architecture, landscape architecture, and horticulture to design a harmonious space. In 2006, workers started removing railroad ties. In 2008, work began on paths and seating, lighting, and various gardens.

Section 1 of the new High Line opened in 2009; Section 2 opened in 2011. Visitors now enjoy a roof-height view of the city as they stroll down a wooden path, observing plants and birds. There are areas for musicians and other public performances. The enormous success of this ambitious project has inspired officials in St. Louis, Chicago, and Philadelphia. They are planning similar parks made from obsolete industrial areas.

A President's Home

by Matthew Kahn

Complex Spelling Patterns

curious	generous	luxurious
famous	gracious	obviously

Thomas Jefferson is obviously known as the author of the Declaration of Independence and the third President of the United States. He is also famous as one of the most intellectually curious Presidents. His interests included plants and birds, music, inventions, and architecture.

Jefferson used his knowledge of architecture to design his home, Monticello. He was inspired by the buildings of an Italian architect, Andrea Palladio. The house is located atop a hill on Jefferson's 5,000-acre plantation. It is a gracious building of red brick with a porch supported by four columns. Jefferson originally built the house in 1770. In the 1780s, Jefferson spent a few years in France. On his return, he added several features he had seen in Europe to his home. For example, he added a dome in the shape of an octagon over the porch. The room inside the dome has been restored to its appearance during Jefferson's lifetime. It has yellow walls and a green floor. It can only be reached by a steep, narrow staircase.

Some visitors might think Monticello is not luxurious by today's standards. But it has some charming features. It has a foldable dining table since Jefferson thought that furniture wasted space. The home's beds are in alcoves. Jefferson said, "I cannot live without books," and his well-stocked library supports this.

In 2013, a generous philanthropist contributed $10 million to Monticello. He wants to have the plantation's slave lodgings reconstructed. Many rooms in the main house will also be restored, including upstairs living areas that are now empty.

Games People Play

by Casey Chancen

Morphemes

competitors	incredibly	pleasurable
contemporary	knowledge	represented
imaginary	logical	specifically
imaginations	originated	unhealthy

Long before people played computer games, they played board games. In fact, board games have an incredibly long history: one known game was played in 3500 B.C.! Although each board game has unique features, all board games have certain traits. They are played on a board specifically made for that game. Players use counters or pieces to mark their progress on the board. Most games require a combination of strategy and chance. Rolling counting cubes often provides the chance portion of the game. The games pit two or more competitors in a struggle to reach the game's goal.

One of the first-known board games is an Egyptian game called Senet. A Senet board and pieces were found in the tomb of King Tutankhamen, who lived from 1341 B.C. to 1323 B.C. Senet has a board with 30 squares and two sets of five or more pawns. The game involved rolling counting cubes and therefore a degree of luck. Egyptians felt that winners were smiled upon by the gods. Another board game, checkers, was played in Mesopotamia and in Ancient Egypt as early as 3000 B.C.

The game of Go originated in China in 1046 B.C. and is still played today. It uses a wooden board with a 19-by-19 grid. Players take turns with a set of black or white pieces called stones and try to surround a larger area on the grid than their opponent. Another ancient game popular today is backgammon, played in Iran since around 3000 B.C. It is played on a two-sided board with twelve long triangular shapes on each side. Players roll counting cubes and try to remove their fifteen checkers from the board first, according to the game's rules. Like many favorite board games, backgammon has fairly simple rules. But players can use complex strategies to win.

People still enjoy a very old Indian game, Pachisi. Players move four pieces around a cross-shaped board, competing to complete the circuit first. Indian players used embroidered cloth boards and cowrie, or snail, shells as counting cubes. In the sixteenth century the Indian Emperor Akbar had red and white squares laid in a courtyard and employed servants as playing pieces.

The game that might be called "the king of board games," chess, also originated in the sixth century in India. The pieces represented military divisions: infantry, cavalry, elephants, and chariots. These evolved into the present-day pieces: pawn, knight, bishop, and rook. By 1000, the game had spread to Europe and Russia. Books about chess strategy were published as early as the 1300s. The games of checkers, chess, and Go are in the board game category of "abstract strategy games."

Some more contemporary games have also become world favorites. In 1903, an American, Elizabeth Phillips, created the game of Monopoly. She wanted to use a game format to explain why business monopolies were unhealthy. (In a monopoly, a single person or company dominates the market for a specific product.) This game of buying and selling imaginary properties became popular around the world. The word game Scrabble was invented in 1938 when crossword puzzles were becoming popular.

Experts say that board games increase players' knowledge and logical thinking. They fire up people's imaginations and create pleasurable suspense. Most people think board games are fun! What is your favorite board game?

Once Every Thousand Years

by Brandon Elliott

Morphemes

attractions	reinvented	suspension
entertainment	representing	unfortunately
exhibition	striking	unimpressed
favorite	successful	usefully

When the calendar turned from December 31, 1999, to January 1, 2000, the entire world celebrated. This was not just a new year, decade, or even century. It was the dawn of a new millennium, or thousand-year period. Many cities around the world marked the occasion with new spaces or structures. Some were more successful than others.

In London, the Millennium Dome was built on the Prime Meridian, or zero longitude, from which time is calculated around the world. To honor Greenwich Mean Time, the Millennium Dome has a diameter of 365 meters and twelve support towers representing the months of the year or the hours on the clock. An exhibition, the Millennium Experience, appeared in the dome during 2000. Unfortunately, the public was unimpressed, and the dome is now part of an entertainment complex.

Also in London is the Millennium Bridge, a steel suspension bridge across the Thames River for pedestrians. The bridge is a favorite landmark because it is usefully located near top tourist destinations. The Tate Modern Museum and Shakespeare's Globe Theatre are on one side; St. Paul's Cathedral is on the other.

Across the Atlantic, Millennium Park in Chicago reinvented an area of old rail yards and parking lots. The park was intended to open in 2000 but was not finished until 2004. It is now one of the city's most visited attractions. Its unique art includes a sculpture, *Cloud Gate*, whose shiny surface reflects the city in striking ways. The Crown Fountain features glass towers that display videos. The park also has gardens, a band shell, and a pedestrian bridge.

The Best Reward

by Harry Wilson

Morphemes

accompanied	immediately	undecipherable
detecting	measurements	undoubtedly
detector	miraculously	unexcited
eventually	rapidly	unnoticed
expression	scientific	unusual
extremely	sizable	
frantically	uncovered	

Andy's family was preparing to move into a new house, and Andy accompanied his mom to take measurements of the house's windows. When Mr. Park, the seller, asked Andy about his interests, Andy told him about soccer, baseball, science fiction movies, scientific experiments, and unusual insects. "And metal detecting," Andy added. "My uncle gave me a metal detector. So far I've found seven quarters, fourteen nails, and a fork."

Mr. Park was extremely interested. "You might discover something here: my wife's diamond ring. By the time we realized she'd lost it in the garden, mud had covered the area. If you find the ring, you can keep it."

Searching immediately after the move, Andy found many objects, including $1.77 in coins, but no ring. What nooks or crannies might have gone unnoticed? Andy saw a gully winding down a slope. "If rain carried garden dirt down the gully . . ." Andy thought. He swept the metal detector along the gully until his arm throbbed with pain. When the detector began to beep, Andy rapidly dug a hole. Miraculously, he uncovered a tiny piece of jewelry, muddy and dull, but undoubtedly Mrs. Park's ring.

Andy shouted frantically, "Mr. Park said I could keep it, so I'm rich!" Mom, unexcited, had an undecipherable expression on her face as Andy washed the ring. Eventually the diamond glistened, and suddenly its sparks seemed to penetrate his brain: he must return the ring. A day later, everyone was satisfied: Mrs. Park had her lost ring, Andy's mom was proud of her son, and Andy had a sizable cash reward in his college savings account.

Aloha, Hawaii!

by Lawrence Klamas

Prefixes *over-*, *in-*

incomparable	overdue	overthrown
incredibly	overlook	overtook
independent	overthrow	overwhelmingly
injustice		

March 12, 1959, was a thrilling day in Hawaii. Hawaiians celebrated with parades, dancing, and ringing bells. The United States House of Representatives had voted to admit Hawaii as the fiftieth state of the Union.

From 1810 until 1893, Hawaii was a kingdom. In 1893, Queen Lili'uokalani was overthrown. Hawaii was led by a newly formed government that wanted Hawaii to be part of the United States. An American diplomat helped plan the overthrow. (One hundred years later, the United States Government apologized for the injustice of this event.) In 1894, Hawaii became an independent republic. In 1898, Hawaii became part of the United Stsates, the Territory of Hawaii.

On December 7, 1941, an event that changed history occurred in Hawaii. Japan bombed the U.S. Naval Base at Pearl Harbor in Honolulu. This attack prompted the United States to join World War II. Americans could not overlook Hawaii's value as a military post. The island of Oahu was the military command center for the Pacific during the war.

After the war, many Americans thought Hawaiian statehood was overdue. Hawaiians overwhelmingly supported statehood. They passed out buttons and stickers calling Hawaii "The 49th State." But not until 1959 did Congress pass the Hawaii Admission Act. (Alaska overtook Hawaii on the road to statehood. It became the 49th state on January 3, 1959.)

The day the act was passed, *The Honolulu Advertiser* wrote, "Every church bell in town will begin pealing. Every ship in harbor will blow her whistle. Most folks will do a little shouting of their own, and, of course, there's nothing to stop you from hula-ing in the streets if you want to." People did hula, and jitterbug, as Dixieland bands played. Thousands of school kids recited "The Pledge of Allegiance" together.

Despite the spirited celebrations, Hawaii did not officially become a state until August 21, 1959. Then President Dwight D. Eisenhower signed an official proclamation. That is why Hawaii celebrates Statehood Day the third Friday in August every year. After making statehood a reality, President Eisenhower directed that a new American flag be made. It would have 50 stars and replace the now outdated flag.

After gaining statehood, Hawaii grew and became more modern. It became an incredibly popular vacation spot. Since 1959, tourism has been Hawaii's largest industry. People from all over the world are delighted by Hawaii's warm climate and natural beauty. Hawaii became part of the United States, but the state kept many incomparable customs. It is still known for graceful hula dances, fragrant flower *leis*, colorful *muumuus*, and *aloha* shirts.

Harry Owens, a Hawaiian, wrote a song about Hawaii's statehood. It went:
"Hawaii is the fiftieth star in the U.S.A.
Aloha means how joyful we are
For at last we are brothers today.
We know that you'll be happy
When Hawaii falls in line.
We sing a song of gladness as we
Join the forty-nine."

"Extra, Extra!"

by Louis Harrison

> **Prefixes over-, in-**
>
> inconceivable   indispensable   overused
>
> indescribable   overeager

"This is breaking news." This overused announcement on television or radio is the twenty-first century's way of announcing an extraordinary event. In previous centuries, you would have been learned of important news from a newsboy selling newspapers. Out on the street, the newsboys would cry, "Extra, extra, read all about it!"

The U.S. Constitution was signed by delegates to the Constitutional Convention on September 17, 1787. On September 22, the *Maryland Gazette* published the document in an extra edition. Historians agree that "extra" editions got their name from the word *extraordinary*. For example, extra editions reported the indescribable news of Lincoln's assassination on April 14, 1865. On December 7, 1941, the *Honolulu Star-Bulletin* published an extra about the inconceivable bombing of Pearl Harbor.

Extra editions served several purposes. First, before radio and television, they were indispensable in delivering important information. Second, they helped publishers make money by beating competitors to big news. Finally, they were a way to commemorate important events.

Most cities insisted that newsboys could sell extras on the street only between 6:00 A.M. and 8:00 P.M. But many an overeager seller broke these rules during events such as the end of World War II. You won't hear many cries of "Extra, extra!" today, but you can still find extra editions describing key events, such as the first election of President Barack Obama in 2008.

An Eerie Trek

by Liz Stellen

Prefixes over-, in-

inexperienced	invisible	overjoyed
inseparable	overcast	overtaken
insufficient	overconfident	

Will and his older brother Grant were inseparable. So when Grant proposed a long hike on Miller Mountain, Will eagerly agreed. Dad dropped them at the trailhead, reminding them to observe the rules of hiking safety.

Will followed Grant energetically up the incline. The day was pleasantly warm; the only music was the buzzing and chirping of forest creatures. Two hours later, at the top of the tall hill, the boys found a handy fallen log and sat down for lunch. They had risen to begin their downhill trek when the eeriest thing happened.

One minute the hill was in warm sunlight; the next, an immense, chilly fog bank had overtaken it. It looked as though Grant was encased in cotton, and the forest and trail were completely invisible. Grant said, "Fog strikes suddenly at this altitude, but it will disappear just as fast. We'll sit here until it recedes."

Will soon began to shiver, his light jacket providing insufficient warmth in the damp fog. The boys silently watched clouds of fog flow around them. After a seeming eternity, Will began to doubt his brother's assessment of the situation. Grant was not an inexperienced hiker, but he was sometimes an overconfident one. What if the fog didn't lift all day?

Will closed his eyes; perhaps he slept briefly. When he looked again, the bank of fog had become thin tendrils. Trees were visible, and Grant's blue shirt was as clear as the sky had been earlier. The boys sighed as they trudged down the trail, unperturbed by the overcast skies and occasional fog swirls; at least they could see the trail. At the trailhead, Will smiled; never before had he been so overjoyed to see a worried look on his dad's face.

An Impressive Giant

by Nathan Hamlin

Compound Words

breathtaking	long-lived	someday
commonplace	noteworthy	sometimes
greenhouse	redwood	walkways
highway		

The Northern California coast has many breathtaking sights, such as roads winding around high, rocky cliffs that fall directly into the ocean. One of the most noteworthy natural wonders is the giant redwood tree. The redwood grows naturally only on a narrow strip of coastal land in California.

One hundred and fifty million years ago, ancestors of the redwood were commonplace all over the United States. Giant redwoods require a cool, wet climate. Frequent fog along the northern California coast provides the moisture that makes these trees grow. And how they grow! A redwood may be up to 378 feet tall and 22 feet in diameter. It is the tallest measured tree species in the world. Redwoods may weigh up to 1.6 million pounds. They may live 2,000 years; their average age is 500 to 700 years.

Giant sequoias are similar to redwoods. They grow at a higher elevation, between 5,000 and 7,000 feet. They grow only on the western side of the Sierra Nevada mountains. Sequoias do not grow as tall as redwoods although their trunks may have a larger diameter, up to 40 feet.

There are several magnificent places to view redwood trees. U.S. Route 101 north of San Francisco is called the Redwood Highway. As it winds north toward Oregon, the highway passes within feet of enormous redwoods. Redwood National Park stretches for 50 miles, beginning 325 miles north of San Francisco. Nearly half of the protected old-growth redwoods grow in the 132,000 acres of this park. Another awe-inspiring redwood forest is on the Big Sur coast, 150 miles south of San Francisco.

Just north of San Francisco, Muir Woods contains thousands of old-growth redwoods. Visitors can stroll on walkways among the trees. In 1908, William and Elizabeth Kent donated this forest to the federal government. They named it after John Muir, who worked to preserve wilderness lands in the West. He was a naturalist who was sometimes called "The Father of the National Parks." Muir was thrilled when the woods became a national monument. He said, "This is the best tree-lovers' monument that could possibly be found in all the forests of the world."

One reason redwoods are long-lived is that they have no natural enemies such as termites. They rarely contract fungal diseases. In fact, humans are the main enemy of redwoods. The reddish-brown bark of the redwood is valued for home building and furniture. So cutting down the trees for lumber has resulted in much of the destruction of the trees.

The giant redwoods of California will someday be growing in Australia, Great Britain, Ireland, Canada, Germany, and various locations in the United States. A nonprofit group has cloned redwoods from three California trees cut down many years ago. They are planting the 18-inch clones in these locations to help fight climate change. Redwoods, because of their gigantic size, can absorb much carbon dioxide. Carbon dioxide causes the greenhouse effect and therefore climate change.

Our Fashion Capital

by Jennifer Wiley

Compound Words

headquarters	ready-made	sometimes
marketplace	showrooms	warehouses

Have you ever visited the New York City neighborhood between 5th and 9th Avenues and between 34th and 42nd Streets? If you do, you might glimpse warehouses, showrooms, and workers related to the fashion industry. This area of Manhattan is known as the garment district.

Until the early 1800s, most American clothing was made at home or by tailors. Then New York clothing makers began producing garments for a few groups: sailors, western prospectors, and plantation owners who needed clothes for enslaved workers. After the sewing machine was invented in the 1850s, the number of clothing manufacturers increased. More and more Americans bought ready-made clothes. Many immigrants from Europe had fashion industry experience. They strengthened the business, so that by 1900, fashion was the city's largest industry.

In the first half of the 20th century, the garment district was bustling. It was headquarters for fashion designers, textile and clothing manufacturers, and related businesses such as zipper makers. However, in recent decades, garment district manufacturing has declined because we live in a world marketplace. Manufacturers can sometimes make their products more cheaply in other countries.

Today, people in the clothing business fight to keep the New York garment district busy. It generates over $14 billion annually. Events such as Fashion Week, in September and in February, boosts the entire New York economy. New Yorkers and all Americans are proud to call New York the fashion capital of the world.

The Election

by Kristen Kensington

Compound Words

brainstormed	loudspeaker	something
brand-new	outdoor	supermarket
everyone	popcorn	worthwhile
however	salespeople	

Tamara loved politics; her heroes were Franklin Roosevelt and Martin Luther King Jr. She knew the names of her state's senators and representatives the President's cabinet, and the Supreme Court justices. So when Polk School announced an election for school president, Tamara signed up immediately. She was soon campaigning against her friend Ben. The principal said the candidates' platforms should be based on a specific issue: the school-wide volunteer activity for the coming year. After Tamara had brainstormed and devised a plan, she wrote her campaign speech.

On campaign speech day, Ben spoke to the assembly. "I think we should sell popcorn in front of the supermarket. Then we can donate the money to the community center so it can improve programs for kids our age." The audience applauded the plan enthusiastically.

Now it was Tamara's turn. "Ben's idea is excellent. However, some students are not good salespeople. I propose we improve the park across the street. We will form three student groups to do different jobs: cleaning up, growing new plants, or creating signs. Then everyone will do something worthwhile, we'll improve our environment, and we'll have a brand-new area for outdoor activities." As she accepted the students' energetic applause, Tamara knew she had done a good job, but so had Ben. Now it was up to the student body.

The next day the principal congratulated Tamara over the loudspeaker, saying, "Now that you've won the election, Tamara, you must do the hard work: leading the school in the volunteer program you've proposed."

A Great Novelist and Philosopher

by Robert Fairfax

The first published work of Leo Tolstoy, shown here in peasant clothing, was a story about his own childhood.

Words from Russian

babushkas   dacha   steppes

czar

When the subject of extravagantly long, complex novels comes up, people often mention *War and Peace*. This book has well over a thousand pages and 580 characters. It was written by the Russian author Leo Tolstoy, who is often considered one of the world's greatest writers.

Tolstoy was born about 100 miles south of Moscow, Russia, in 1828 to a wealthy, noble family. He was not very interested in formal education and joined the army at the age of twenty-three. His army experience changed his attitude toward life. He became distrustful of governments and hated war.

Tolstoy grew up in a society in which wealthy landowners had serfs. Serfs worked the land, helping landowners grow wealthy, in return for a place to live. Another name for *serf* is *peasant*. Tolstoy's father had serfs; as Tolstoy grew older, he found this system to be immoral. He founded schools to educate the children of peasants. He came to believe that the simple life of peasants, who lived close to nature and did not focus on material possessions, was the ideal way of life.

Tolstoy published *War and Peace* in 1865. It describes historical events during the reign of Czar Alexander I and France's invasion of Russia led by Napoleon in 1812. The characters include the members of several fictional families as well as real people such as Napoleon. One vivid character is Count Pierre Bezukhov, an awkward young man who goes to war. He is modeled in many ways on Tolstoy. Another is Countess Natasha Rostova, a young girl in the beginning of the novel. Tolstoy describes her as "not pretty but full of life." Tolstoy shows how these and many other characters are affected by the war. The scenes of the novel range from battlegrounds to ballrooms. The characters range from peasants wearing babushkas to society ladies in satin gowns.

In the 1870s, Tolstoy became a devout Christian. In 1886 he published a short novel, *The Death of Ivan Ilych*. It tells the story of a wealthy man who focuses on his material possessions, especially his house and its decorations. As he nears death, he regrets the superficial way in which he has lived. Tolstoy said, "Everyone thinks of changing the world, but no one thinks of changing himself."

Tolstoy was happily married and had fourteen children. But he changed as he grew older, and his wife did not share all his beliefs. His works became increasingly focused on his life philosophy. He began dressing in peasant clothing and became a vegetarian. Tolstoy had a *dacha*, or country house, where he enjoyed socializing with peasants. He believed strongly in loving one's neighbor. His ideas about nonviolent resistance influenced Martin Luther King Jr. Tolstoy died in 1910 at the age of eighty-two.

Readers of Tolstoy appreciate many aspects of his works, such as his realistic characters. They enjoy his portraits of many different Russian settings: the sophisticated cities of Moscow and St. Petersburg, rural farms, and distant steppes. Many critics believe that *War and Peace* is one of the top three novels ever written.

The Princess Who Never Smiled:
A Russian Fairy Tale

Retold by Susana Rosenfield

> **Words from Russian**
>
> balalaika   rubles   sable
>
> czar

Euna, a Russian princess, seemed to have everything; however, she never smiled. Euna's misery made her father, the czar, miserable in turn, and he tried desperately to make Euna smile or laugh. He issued a challenge to the kingdom's young men: the one to make Euna happy could marry her. Suitors tried to amuse Euna with everything from magic tricks to balalaika music, but she remained morose.

Across town lived a poor, plain worker. After a prosperous year, his master displayed a basket of rubles, saying, "Take all you please." The humble man took one coin, but when he went to drink at the well, he dropped it. The next year, the worker again took one coin and again accidentally lost it at the well. The third year, the worker took his coin to the well again, but on this occasion when he dropped the coin, his other two coins appeared. The worker took his money on a journey where he met a mouse who begged for help. The worker gave the mouse a coin. Next he met a beetle, to whom he gave his second coin. Finally, he met a catfish and, full of sympathy for the fish, gave it his last coin.

The end of the journey took the penniless worker by the czar's palace where he saw Euna, dressed in silk and sable, staring at him. Disconcerted, he fell into the muddy road, where his friends the mouse, the beetle, and the catfish quickly came to help. The clumsy rescue brought peals of laughter from the princess. When the czar eagerly called for the man who had made Euna laugh, the worker, now transformed into a handsome gentleman, came to the palace. He married the princess, and the pair smiled and laughed forever after.

A Mammoth Beast

by Amelia Torres

Words from Russian

mammoth   steppe(s)   tundra

Have you ever seen an Asian elephant at the zoo? Then you have seen a relative of a prehistoric beast, the woolly mammoth. This animal has been extinct for 10,000 years. In 1796, a French scientist identified the mammoth as an extinct elephant species.

One way people learned of this animal was through pictures. Prehistoric people painted pictures of it in caves. Another is its habitat, the *mammoth steppe*, in North America, Europe, and Asia. Around 20,000 years ago, this was a cold, dry habitat with few trees. Its cold weather and frozen ground preserved many woolly mammoth remains.

The mammoth steppe habitat is also called *steppe-tundra*. It has traits of both biomes. Tundra has some plants but few trees. It is in high latitudes with low temperatures. Steppes are grassy plains with a very dry climate. They have big differences in temperature between summer and winter and between day and night.

The woolly mammoth was protected from the cold by long fur with a shorter layer underneath. It had small ears to reduce heat loss and a shoulder hump that made its back look sloped. It was almost as large as today's African elephants. The animal probably became extinct when the world climate changed and its habitat disappeared. Early humans used mammoths' tusks and bones to make tools. Today people still make objects from ivory left behind by these extinct animals.

Camp Is Terrible

by Lila Rosen

Complex Spelling Patterns: _ci_/sh/, _ti_/sh/, _ous_/us/

cautiously	delicious	outrageous
conscious	infectious	precious
curiously	nutritious	spacious

Alicia couldn't believe it when her mom woke her up at 6:00 A.M. It felt as though she had fallen asleep five minutes ago. The day she had dreaded had arrived. She wished she could go on sleeping instead of going to catch the bus to summer camp.

This would be Alicia's first time at camp. Several of her friends had gone for two or three years, and they encouraged her to go too, but Alicia had always said no. Summer was too precious. She liked staying home with her parents, her brother, and Charlie, her dog. She enjoyed the summer activities at home: going to the pool with her friends, eating hamburgers in the backyard, playing softball at the park. She didn't need two weeks at camp to enjoy her summer. But this year her parents had insisted: they had to make a trip to stay with Alicia's grandma, and they thought Alicia would have more fun at camp. Alicia made her parents promise that if she went to camp this once, she would never have to go again.

The butterflies in Alicia's stomach fluttered around all the way to camp. As she met her roommates in her spacious cabin, made her bed, and organized her belongings, she felt a homesick feeling deep inside. How would she endure fourteen days of this?

As the days passed, Alicia became very sure about the things she liked about camp and the things she disliked. She liked hearing the birds sing cheerily when she woke up each morning, but she disliked the spooky rustlings she heard when she went to bed each night. She liked the long hikes through the quiet pine woods, but she disliked swimming lessons in the chilly lake. She liked the delicious raisin-and-nut trail mix they munched on during hikes. She disliked the nutritious but boring oatmeal served instead of her favorite breakfast cereal each morning. She definitely disliked the daddy longlegs that turned up repeatedly in the cabin.

During the last week, Alicia and her cabin mates, like all the other campers, created and practiced a skit for the last night of camp. Her cabin mates' enthusiasm was infectious. They laughed and argued and sang as they practiced their skit. They had so much fun that Alicia was surprised to find that the last day of camp had arrived. Of course, she still couldn't wait to go home; but she was conscious of focusing more on presenting her group's skit that night than on seeing her family tomorrow.

The skit turned out better than Alicia and her group could have hoped. Everyone laughed and clapped, and the campers voted the skit the most outrageous of the night. As the last night of camp came to an end, Alicia realized that she had made friends who were as close as the ones at home. Nodding off to sleep, she was almost sad as she realized that she would never see her camp friends again.

She was saying good-bye to those friends the next day when her parents drove up. Overjoyed, she hugged her mom as though they'd been apart for two months instead of two weeks. As they prepared to go, the head counselor walked up to say good-bye. "Alicia, we'd like you to come back next year as a junior counselor, if you're interested."

Alicia was speechless, so her mom cautiously began, "This year at camp was just an experiment. I'm not sure Alicia—"

"I'd love to!" Alicia finally shouted, as her parents looked at her curiously. "I'll explain on the way home," she said.

The Gourmet Interstate

Paul Baxter

Complex Spelling Patterns: *ci*/sh/, *ti*/sh/, *ous*/us/

ambitious	enormously	nutritious
budget-conscious	luxurious	scrumptious
delicious		

Have you ever bought a frozen treat from an ice cream truck? Then you've participated in the food truck phenomenon, which has become enormously popular in many American cities.

The ancestor of today's food truck is the cowboy chuck wagon. After the Civil War, ranchers moved cattle across land to their customers. The cowboys' chuck wagon followed the trail. It was stocked with dried foods such as beans and bacon. A cook prepared meals on the range for the cowboys. The cowboys' diet was not particularly nutritious, since fresh fruits and vegetables weren't available. However, chuck wagons usefully provided basic meals.

During the 1900s, food trucks catered to customers who needed meals at odd hours or in off-the-beaten-path places. Night food trucks sold meals to night workers. Lunch trucks parked at construction sites, movie sets, and college campuses. Some trucks carried ready-made food. Others had kitchens where chefs cooked fresh meals.

Around 2008, many restaurants had fewer customers because of an economic recession. Food trucks were less luxurious but also cheaper than permanent restaurants. Budget-conscious consumers eagerly bought scrumptious meals at reasonable prices. In big cities, ambitious chefs created unique menus, often offering one type of food such as gourmet tacos or grilled cheese. Business boomed, and now food trucks are fashionable as well as practical. Cities such as New Orleans and Houston have held food truck festivals. Customers check locations of their favorite food trucks on the Internet and enjoy delicious grub all over town.

Nature's Roller Coasters

Andy Naismith

Complex Spelling Patterns: _ci_/sh/, _ti_/sh/, _ous_/us/

anxiously	famous	marvelous
cautiously	gracious	repetitious
contentious	luxurious	spacious

The Robinson family was planning a special trip. However, they couldn't agree on where to go. James wanted to ride roller coasters at a famous theme park and stay in a luxurious resort. His sister Holly wanted to go to the beach. After a contentious discussion, Dad said he'd pick a destination out of a hat.

Dad chose a slip of paper and said, "Montana it is!" Dad wanted to enjoy Montana's spacious plains and go fly-fishing. He wanted to hike in Glacier National Park. James was disappointed. He didn't want to go on repetitious nature hikes. He longed to ride a huge roller coaster and get frightened in a haunted house.

In Montana, the family stayed in a gracious lodge in an evergreen forest. The first day, the family went to a wide river. After handing out lifejackets and helmets, a guide led the way to a large rubber raft. The guide and the Robinsons boarded the boat and began drifting down the calm river. Soon James felt choppy waves and saw white water. The guide kept the raft upright as it rose and plunged in the rough current. After the bumpy ride, James and Holly chatted excitedly about the unexpected thrills.

The next day, the family saw lakes like mirrors and snow-covered peaks at Glacier National Park. Dad drove cautiously along the Going to the Sun Road. James gazed anxiously below the road to canyons and valleys far below.

James had a marvelous vacation. Maybe next year he would enjoy the thrills of a theme park. But this year he appreciated the natural excitement of Montana.

A 20th Century Artist

by Will Owens

Georgia O'Keeffe painted *Petunias* in 1925.

Word Families

art/artist(s)/artistic

created/creative

energetic/energy

impressed/
impression

memorable/
remember(ed)

student/studied

You've probably seen at least one of this artist's paintings. Perhaps it was a huge, brilliant reddish orange blossom, or a 1920s skyscraper against a dark city sky. After viewing one of her works, you will probably always remember the vivid art of Georgia O'Keeffe.

Georgia O'Keeffe was born in Wisconsin in 1887. She was an artistic child. At eighteen, she attended the School of the Art Institute in Chicago and later the Art Students League in New York City. During these years, 1905–1908, young artists were taught a realistic style of painting. O'Keeffe decided she could never succeed at it. She left school and didn't paint for four years.

Fortunately, O'Keeffe took a summer school class at the University of Virginia. There she studied a different painting philosophy. The painter Arthur Wesley Dow believed an artist should use shape, color, and shading to reflect his or her emotions. Later in her life O'Keeffe said, "I found I could say things with color and shapes that I couldn't say any other way—things I had no words for." Inspired, she created several charcoal drawings. They were seen by an important New York art expert, Alfred Stieglitz. The energetic, swirling shapes of the drawings impressed Stieglitz, and he displayed them in his gallery. In 1918, O'Keeffe moved to New York and began painting full-time. In the mid-1920s, she painted the dramatic skyscraper pictures, which became one of her trademarks. Her art made an impression on art lovers and critics alike.

A turning point in O'Keeffe's art occurred when she visited New Mexico in 1929. She began to paint the Western landscape and adobe buildings. She also created still lifes with objects such as animal skulls. She painted a small adobe mission church built in the 1700s in Ranchos de Taos. O'Keeffe thought it was one of the most beautiful buildings left by the Spaniards. She painted it many times. She spent part of every year until 1949 in New Mexico and in 1949 moved there permanently. Known to some extent as a loner, she lived in a small town 50 miles north of Santa Fe until she died in 1986. She was 98.

O'Keeffe's reputation has grown since her death. If you ask art lovers to describe a memorable O'Keeffe painting, they might mention the energy of her bright flowers—poppies, petunias, or calla lilies. They might mention a New York City skyscraper, a Western landscape, or a blue sky dotted with white clouds. She is known for all of these works of art. She is also remembered as an independent artist with an original creative vision.

Georgia O'Keeffe's paintings are displayed at many museums including New York's Museum of Modern Art and Chicago's Art Institute. You can also see them at the Georgia O'Keeffe Museum in Santa Fe, New Mexico, which opened in 1997. It has over 1,000 paintings, drawings, and sculptures by O'Keeffe. It is the world's only museum devoted to an American female artist known throughout the world.

Dad's Time Machine

by Jim Foxx

Word Families

aware/wary	bumpier/bumpy	impatient/patient
awed/awesome	fortunate/fortunes	prepared/preparing
believe/unbelievably		

The airplane had sat on the runway for two hours. Sam already felt bored, antsy, impatient, and ready to exit the plane. Yet he and Dad hadn't even begun the four-hour flight from St. Louis to San Francisco. "I wish we lived in the old days, Dad," he said, "so we could ride a stagecoach to San Francisco. That would have been unbelievably awesome."

"Let's get on the time machine, go back about a hundred years, and take the stagecoach. Here we are, in 1900; the stagecoach has been running from St. Louis to San Francisco since at least 1849, when Gold Rushers went to make their fortunes. We'd better be patient and prepared for a long trip since we're going five miles an hour, and if we're fortunate the trip will take only twenty-two days. We're squeezed in this tiny compartment on a hard bench with another person and with six people on the other seats. The dirt road is bumpy, so every time we hit a rut, we bounce like crazy. Soon we'll reach the next stage so the driver can change horses, and we can stretch our legs. Let's hope the driver doesn't leave without us, or we could be stranded here for days waiting for a coach that has space.

"We'd better be wary of highway bandits, too, and hope the driver can protect us. Let's hope the weather stays good; if it rains, these roads will turn to mud and our trip will be even slower and bumpier—if we make it at all. It's an awesome trip, isn't it, Sam?"

"I'm suddenly aware that I'm completely awed by this airplane. I believe it's preparing to take off, Dad."

"The Sun Will Come Out Tomorrow"

by Ella Sampson

Word Families

adventurous/ adventures

appearances/ appeared

imaginations/ imaginative

inspiration/ inspired

wondered/ wonderful

Have you ever wondered where the writers of plays and movies get their ideas? Of course, they use their imaginations. Sometimes, however, they are inspired by reality or by works in other genres. For example, the musical *The Sound of Music* was based on the true story of a singing family in Austria in the 1940s. Another musical that had an unusual origin is *Annie*.

"Little Orphan Annie" was a comic strip written by Harold Gray. It first appeared in 1924, in an era when newspaper comics were widely read. Annie, an 11-year-old orphan, was one of the few females to be the main character in a comic strip at that time. Annie, with her trademark curly red hair, has a dog, Sandy. Her friend, the wealthy "Daddy" Warbucks, helps care for her. Although Annie's adventures were often implausible, Annie remained a sensible, optimistic girl. A poll in 1937 found that "Little Orphan Annie" was America's favorite comic strip.

In 1930, "Little Orphan Annie" became a radio show. Then it was made into films in 1932 and 1938. Flash forward to 1977: "Little Orphan Annie" was the inspiration for the musical play *Annie*. This show became wildly popular. It played on Broadway until 1983 and was also produced in hundreds of other theaters. In 1982 *Annie* became a well-received film and was filmed again in 1999. Annie truly has had a wonderful life. The comic strip was canceled in 2010, but adults and children alike know Annie from one of her many appearances. She's the adventurous, imaginative girl who says "Leapin' lizards" and sings about hope for "Tomorrow."

Ana Garcia, Cub Reporter

by Maria Acuna

A visitor reads front page news from newspaper pages displayed
outdoors at the Newseum.

Compound Words

byline	nearby	someplace
bystanders	newspapers	something
classroom	notebook	weekend
firefighter	outdoor	

When Ana's family went to Washington, D.C., they saw impressive sights: the White House, the Capitol, the Washington Monument. But Ana's favorite place was the Newseum, a museum devoted to coverage of news events by newspapers, radio, and television. Ana was captivated by the outdoor display of the day's front pages from newspapers around the country. Inside, she was enthralled by the exhibit of front pages recording momentous events dating back to the 1700s.

Ana determined that day to become a news reporter and began contemplating how to reach her goal. She decided to start by writing stories for the town newspaper; she just needed a story to report. Ana studied the weekly paper, filled with articles on local sports, car accidents, and musical events. She saw an announcement of a town council meeting on Monday and decided this would be her first assignment.

On Monday evening, Ana sat with her dad in the town hall meeting room, notebook and pen at the ready. As the council members discussed zoning regulations, Ana sat, her pen poised above her notebook, waiting for a significant development. The zoning discussion went on and on. "What's Ordinance 23A, Dad?" she asked. Dad put his finger to his lips. Ana thought she'd take notes as soon as something interesting was discussed. However, after two hours her notebook remained empty. Ana decided to search for news someplace else.

The next day, three fire trucks passed Ana and her older brother as they walked home from school. She persuaded Marco to help her investigate, and on the next block, they saw black smoke and flames streaming from a house. Notebook and pen in hand, she approached a firefighter to ask how the fire had started.

"Move back, young lady," the man said. "This is a dangerous situation." Next Ana asked some bystanders for information, but they knew as little as she. Ana watched until the fire was extinguished, but she discovered no remarkable news to report.

"Mom, becoming a reporter is difficult," she said at home. "There are no important events around here, and if there were, no one would give the story to a twelve-year-old reporter."

After a while Mom said, "I know someone interesting that you might interview, and you might be surprised at the story she can tell."

That weekend Mom took Ana to a house in a nearby neighborhood. When an elderly woman opened the door, Mom said, "Ana, this is Mrs. Morgan, who was my fifth-grade teacher. She taught at Lincoln School for forty-two years, beginning in 1960."

Ana had a list of questions ready, and for the next two hours Mrs. Morgan told Ana fascinating things about her teaching career. Mrs. Morgan reminisced about watching the first trips into space on a classroom television and learning with her students that President Kennedy had been assassinated. She proudly said that one of her students had become a Supreme Court Justice, one had become a governor, three had become members of Congress, and two had become Hollywood actors. "But I remember all my students," Mrs. Morgan said, "not just the ones who became famous. Every individual student taught me something while I was teaching him or her."

Two weeks later, Ana's story appeared in the local paper: "'Local and National History Seen Through the Eyes of Area Teacher'" by Ana Garcia." Her first byline! Ana's journalism career had officially begun.

The Language of Sports

by Theo Brenton

Compound Words

baseball	football	salesperson
everyday	outfield	something
everyone	quarterback	widespread

Human beings like to use colorful language. As soon as people created languages, they likely used figures of speech. A figure of speech expresses an idea in a nonliteral way. Some figures of speech have come to have widespread usage.

Many common figures of speech come from sports. A friend might say, "I haven't started my science project yet. Now I'm behind the eight ball." The expression "behind the eight ball" comes from the game of pool, probably a game in which a player had poor chances if he or she was assigned certain balls with high numbers.

Professional football games are usually played on Sundays. The day after the game, everyone has an opinion about how the games should have been played. That's why a person who proclaims how something should have been done after the fact is called a "Monday morning quarterback."

Baseball has given rise to numerous figures of speech. In a baseball stadium, the outfield—right, center, and left—is the area most distant from home plate. So when someone shares an idea that seems to come from the middle of nowhere, it's said to be right out of left field. When a batter misses the ball three times, he's called out. So a salesperson who can't persuade a customer to make a big purchase might say she "struck out." If the salesperson does make the big sale, she hit a home run. Or, to use a golfing figure of speech, she got a hole in one.

You can use colorful language including sports figures of speech in everyday conversations as well as writing for school. Go ahead. As a tennis player would say, the ball's in your court.

Help Around the House

by Clarisse Bailey

Compound Words

backyard	homemakers	iceboxes
dishwashers	homemaking	washboard
great-grandparents	household	widespread
	housework	

Homemaking today involves many chores. You may think the work is tedious. But if you had lived in your great-grandparents' time, you would have found the chores harder. Many appliances were invented in the 20th century that made housework easier.

In the early 1900s, most Americans washed clothes by hand in a sink. They used a washboard, a rectangular wooden tool with ridges, to help remove dirt. After washing clothes, people had to wring them to remove excess water. This job became easier when the electric wringer was invented. It had two drums through which clothes were fed to squeeze out excess water. Even after electric washing machines became common, dryers were not. Homemakers often hung laundry on lines in the backyard to dry. The electric dryer was invented in 1938.

Refrigerating food was also not easy or efficient. In the early 1900s people had iceboxes. These were cabinets, often wooden, with an ice compartment. Blocks of ice for iceboxes were delivered by an "ice man." Homemakers had to empty the melted ice and replace it with solid ice regularly. Electric refrigerators were invented in 1913 and became widespread in the 1920s. Only in the last half of the century did most people have fridges that kept foods fresh for a lengthy time. With better cooling, homemakers could shop for groceries less often.

Electric dishwashers were invented in the 1920s, but many Americans did not have them until the 1970s. All these appliances have made household chores easier for busy families.

A Famous Architect

by Bridget Riley

The Walt Disney Concert Hall in Los Angeles is one of architect Frank Gehry's designs.

Homographs

impressed	school	size
match	scraps	well
refuse		

You probably know the names of many artists, such as Renoir, Van Gogh, and Picasso. But you may not know the names of any architects. Although architects are a sort of artist, they usually are not well-known.

An architect designs buildings. Being an architect requires many different skills and talents. An architect must be artistic to design aesthetically pleasing structures. But he or she must also understand the technical aspects of buildings. Frank Gehry is an architect who has become well-known all over the world for his spectacular buildings.

Frank Gehry was born in Canada in 1929. As a child, he and his grandmother built little houses and cities out of wood scraps. In 1947, Gehry moved to California. He was not sure what he wanted to do for a living or what he was good at. Recalling activities he enjoyed, he thought about building houses with his grandmother. He ended up graduating from the School of Architecture at the University of California.

The first Gehry-designed building that attracted attention was his own home, a pink cottage in Santa Monica, California, that he remodeled in 1978. He put a new, artistic exterior of metal, glass, and wood on the house but let the old exterior show as well. In 1993, Gehry designed the Frederick R. Weisman Art Museum at the University of Minnesota. One side of the building is brick and is similar to other buildings on campus.

But the other side of the building does not match. It is covered with a festival of curved stainless steel shapes. It is an abstract representation of a waterfall.

The Dancing House is an office building in Prague that Gehry designed in 1992. The curved, lopsided structure looks like two figures dancing. It is made of concrete panels of a variety of shapes and sizes.

The building that impressed many people and made Gehry famous the world over was the Guggenheim Museum in Bilbao, an industrial city on a river in northeastern Spain. Gehry created a fantastic structure covered with randomly placed titanium sheets. Titanium is a strong, shiny silver metal. Many critics called the building, with its vaguely ship-like shape, a masterpiece. One called it "the greatest building of our time." The building opened in 1997, and the city's economy immediately improved. Gehry's building became a major tourist attraction.

Another successful Gehry building is the Walt Disney Concert Hall in downtown Los Angeles, completed in 2003. It is covered in curved stainless steel shapes. Gehry is attracted to fish shapes, and he designed a huge fish sculpture in the Olympic Village in Barcelona, Spain, in 1992.

Because Gehry's buildings are so unusual, they sometimes cause controversy. Some experts think that some Gehry design elements are wasteful because they do not serve a purpose for their buildings. Others have said that the structures stand out preposterously in their surroundings. They refuse to see the buildings as works of art. But most people who have viewed a Gehry building would agree that it is a fascinating work of art.

Surf's Up

by Ken Bellin

Homographs

arms	resume	swell
desert	school	watch
fell	shore	

Jon loved visiting his young, energetic Uncle Matt in Southern California. Matt, a champion surfer, had won competitions from the Pipeline in Hawaii to Bells Beach in Australia. One day Jon and Uncle Matt, toting his surfboard beneath his arm, strolled to the beach. "This is the birthplace of surfing in the States," Uncle Matt said. "George Freeth grew up surfing in Hawaii. In 1907, he was hired by a big developer in this area to entertain folks with surfing."

Jon watched from the beach as Uncle Matt straddled his board and paddled out to the calm ocean, where an occasional large wave rolled in. Uncle Matt waited patiently, and when a sizeable swell thundered toward shore, he clambered to his feet. He gracefully rode the wave in, using his arms for balance, and fell gently off the board as the wave died; his timing, balance, and strength were amazing.

Uncle Matt, all smiles, yelled, "Now it's your turn!" Jon was taken aback; he had only come to watch his uncle. He was a good swimmer, but he hated saltwater, and the idea of being tossed about in a wave was very disagreeable. Matt called, "Come on, it's not like we're going big-wave surfing. The ocean's like glass today."

Waving, Jon was ready to desert the beach and turned to go home. He was both embarrassed and annoyed. If he'd known Uncle Matt wanted him to *participate* . . . Jon caught himself. Was he afraid of a challenge? He retraced his steps, and two hours and innumerable tumbles later, Jon had ridden four waves. When Matt declared the lesson over and suggested tacos for lunch, Jon made him promise to resume surf school the very next day.

The Cuddly Koala

by Jess Selen

Homographs

die	live	minute
down	long	story
fast		

The koala is one of the world's most appealing animals. It is small, only thirty-three inches long and thirty-three pounds at the largest. It has soft fur, fuzzy ears, and a button nose. Until recently, the koala was not endangered. Its story teaches a critical lesson.

Koalas live only on the continent of Australia, in coastal areas. They eat eucalyptus trees, so they live in woodland habitats. Koalas may sleep for 20 hours a day because their diet has few nutrients. They are marsupials. Mothers give birth to minute, underdeveloped babies. The babies mature in the mother's pouch for six to seven months.

In the early 20th century, koalas were hunted and sold for their fur. They nearly died out. Conservationists made an outcry, and the population increased.

The International Union for Conservation of Nature studies animal populations to see whether they are in danger of extinction. In 2008, the Union was not concerned about the koala. It had large populations that were not dying out too fast. But in 2012 the Australian government found that the koala populations were dying out quickly in some regions. They said koalas were vulnerable: they could become endangered.

The main reason for declining koala populations is deforestation. Builders cut down eucalyptus trees on valued coastal land, and farmers cut down trees to sell for lumber. Without the eucalyptus forest habitat, koalas will die out. But with a "vulnerable" status, koalas will be protected by stricter laws. Also, there are special protected areas for koalas and other endangered animals.

Acknowledgments

Photographs:

2 Ed Merritt/DK Images; **4** Peter Dennis/DK Images; **9** abxyz/ Shutterstock; **11** Brandon Bourdages/Shutterstock; **17** eddtoro/ Shutterstock; **19** Kevin Schafer/Alamy; **25** Aletia/Shutterstock; **26** Oscar Espinosa/Shutterstock; **33** Bettmann/CORBIS; **35** Bettmann/ CORBIS; **41** Mirvav/Shutterstock; **43** arqphotography/Fotolia; **49** Jeff Greenberg/Alamy; **51** Steve Debenport/Getty Images; **57** Charles O. Cecil/Alamy; **59** Stocktrek Images/Getty Images; **65** ©NASA Archive/Alamy; **67** Image Asset Management Ltd./Alamy; **73** Library of Congress—edited version © Science Faction/Getty Images; **75** Ivan Cholakov/Shutterstock; **81** Jeff Greenough/Alamy; **84** vm/Getty Images; **89** Deborah Kolb/Shutterstock; **91** Mirjana Jovic/Getty Images; **97** Jgz/Fotolia; **99** Marcus Lindström/Getty Images; **105** Michael Nicholson/Corbis; **107** CBW/Alamy; **113** JJ pixs/Shutterstock; **115** CTK/Alamy; **121** D Alderman/Alamy; **123** Photo Researchers/Alamy; **129** Kumar Sriskandan/Alamy; **132** Sean Justice/Corbis; **137** Greer Studios/Corbis; **139** Kurt Krieger/ Corbis.